THE NEW INCUBATION BOOK
the essential reference guide

THE NEW INCUBATION BOOK
the essential reference guide

Dr. A. F. Anderson Brown, M.A., M.B., B.Chir., D.R.C.O.G.
and
G. E. S. Robbins

hancock
house

Published simultaneously in Canada and the United States by
HANCOCK HOUSE PUBLISHERS LTD.
19313 Zero Avenue, Surrey, B.C. Canada V3Z 9R9
(604) 538-1114   Fax (604) 538-2262
HANCOCK HOUSE PUBLISHERS
#104-4550 Birch Bay-Lynden Rd, Blaine, WA, U.S.A. 98230-9436
(800) 938-1114   Fax (800) 983-2262
www.hancockhouse.com   sales@hancockhouse.com

CONTENTS

v

LIST OF ILLUSTRATIONS

Product manufacturers

A.B.Incubators
Unit 1, Church Farm, Chelmondiston, Suffolk IP9 1HS
   England.
Tel/Fax 00 44 1473 780050.
E-mail: richard@abincubators.fsnet.co.uk
   www.abincubators.co.uk

Avitronics
Rose in Valley, Lower Hugus Road, Threemilestone,
Truro.Cornwall. TR3 6BD England
Tel/Fax 00 44 1872 262777
E-mail: avitronics@globalnet.co.uk

Brinsea Products Ltd.
Station Road, Sandford, North Somerset. BS25 5RA England
Tel. 00 44 1934 823039. Fax. 00 44 1934 820250
E-mail: sales@brinsea.co.uk
   www.brinsea.co.uk

or

Brinsea Products Inc.
704 North Dixie Avenue, Titusville, FL 32796, USA
Tel. (321) 267 7009. Fax. (321) 267 6090.
E-mail: BrinseaFL@aol.com

Marcon Gamestock Ltd.
Flaxton, Nr York, Yorkshire, YO6 7PZ, England
Tel. 00 44 1904 468588. Fax. 00 44 1904 468678

Sunrise Aviculture
Main Street, Bramley, Rotherham, South Yorkshire S66 0SE
   England
Tel/Fax 00 44 1709 545619.
   www.sunriseaviculture.co.uk

ACKNOWLEDGEMENTS

We would particularly like to thank the following people for their help in preparing this latest revised edition:

Brian Pillow – who provided the information on his commercial partridge hatchery

Pat Corder – for proof reading the original new copy

John Corder – for helping to revise and computerise this edition

Dr. Charles Deeming – for help with the incubation of Ratites

Richard Edgell – for the latest information on incubator manufacture for exotic species

Keith Howman – President of WPA, for his and the Association's support in publishing this revised edition.

Dr Miranda Stevenson – in helping with data for penguins

Jim Reeve of Avitronics -for information regarding the Buddy Candler

INTRODUCTION

During the 20 years since the publication of the first edition of this book, natural habitat has been lost at a far greater rate than ever envisaged. The collection of wild specimens to replace captive losses has virtually ceased due to public pressure, and some countries have now totally banned the practice.

Several reintroduction projects, from captive stock, are underway. It is imperative that a wider diversity of bird and reptile propagation is mastered to ensure the survival of ailing populations. To this end, new chapters have been added to cover the incubation and hatching of high value eggs, and to advise on the latest techniques for species needing specialist treatment. Where appropriate, the latest advances in incubation and rearing equipment have also been included.

So wrote Arthur Anderson Brown before his untimely death in 1991, by which time he had updated his original text and left notes on new photographs he wanted included. His close friend and colleague, Gary Robbins, worked with him for many years on the design and improvement of his incubators; these were to become some of the most advanced models in the world for rare and endangered species. Gary kindly agreed to complete the 1st revision in 1994, and he published a further update in 1999.

With some practical experience from another of Arthur's friends, Rob Harvey, Gary Robbins has written new chapters on incubation techniques since the turn of the millennium and has included details for specific species. Rob Harvey has kindly allowed the use of some of his tables and photographs from his own book Practical Incubation (1990). Much of the research for the Practical Incubation book was carried out on incubators designed by Arthur Anderson Brown and built by A.B. Incubators Ltd., of which he was a founding Director. The World Pheasant Association is publishing this new and completely revised edition, and would like to acknowledge and thank Gary Robbins, the Consultant to A.B. Incubators, for the many long hours he has put into revising this book. WPA would also like to thank Rob Harvey for his kind help. We are sure that Arthur Anderson Brown, whose original book is called by many "The bible of

1

incubation", would have been pleased to see the continuation of the traditions that he started.

Every egg is valuable, and successful incubation depends on a potentially hatchable egg. Knowledge of the basic processes that occur during the transition from egg to chick is essential for the proper management of incubation, whether it be in a machine or under a broody hen. The physical conditions that cause this development to proceed must be understood. Knowing why certain things are done leads to a better understanding of how they are done, and these then lead to an improvement in results. The knowledge of why things went wrong prevents the same mistake being repeated.

In the seven years since this book was revised, we have seen many additions to the number of species now being artificially incubated, which in turn has introduced new techniques in egg turning, humidity control and microprocessor programming of temperatures, which all go together to achieve the ultimate incubation success.

May 2002.

Chapter 1

THE STRUCTURE OF THE EGG

"Which came first, the chicken or the egg?" is a question that has amused the thinking man for centuries. On the assumption that it was the chicken, the egg can be described as a plan, or blueprint, of another chicken, with sufficient building materials to make it. Should the plan be faulty, or the building materials inadequate, it will not produce another chicken.

The basic structure of all eggs is the same. They differ only in the blueprint inside them, and the proportions of the various constituents. For all practical purposes, the egg consists of five principal parts: the shell, its membranes and air space, the white or albumen, the yolk, and the germinal disc.

THE GERMINAL DISC

This is the plan of the future bird. In a broken-out hen's egg, it can be seen as a white spot on top of the yolk, about 4mm in diameter. It is formed by the union of a single cell produced in the ovary of the female with a single sperm produced by the male. The female cell contains half the total number of chromosomes (the genetic instructions) and the male cell the other half. After fusion, or fertilisation, of the two halves the resultant cell divides into two, and these two cells grow and divide again and again until, by the time the egg is laid, the mass of cells is visible as the germinal disc. During incubation, this mass of cells will further grow, divide, and specialise to form the resultant chick, using the remainder of the egg contents as food.

THE YOLK

The yolk is also formed in the ovary, together with the female germ cell. It consists of a delicate spherical sac, the vitelline membrane, which encloses the female germ cell, and a vast store of food reserve.

The food reserve is composed of 50% water, 30% fat and 20% protein. The majority of this food reserve is not used during incubation, but is drawn into the abdominal cavity of the chick just before hatching, and is used to sustain it in the first few days of life.

Those birds which hatch well developed, active and mobile, such as pheasants, ducks, chicken and geese, have a relatively large yolk in proportion to the rest of the egg, whilst those that hatch blind, naked and helpless, have a relatively small yolk.

THE WHITE OR ALBUMEN
This is the principle store for food and water in the egg, and is completely used up during incubation. It consists of 10% protein, the rest being water, and is deposited round the yolk in the upper part of the oviduct. It contains the water-soluble vitamins and minerals, while the yolk contains the fat-soluble ones.

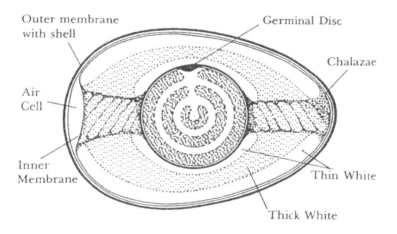

Fig. 1.1 Longitudinal section through a egg

The albumen is not of uniform consistency throughout. Part of it is thick and jelly-like, and part is thin and watery. The thick albumen has a function apart from food value, as suspensory ligaments and shock absorber for the yolk. The yolk is less dense than the albumen and, were it not for these restraining mechanisms, it would float to the top of the egg and stick to the shell. This does indeed happen if the egg is stored too long without turning.

A very thin film of dense white surrounds the yolk. Attached to this, opposite each end of the egg, are suspensory ligaments, or chalazae. These are spring-like coils of thick white, coiling in opposite directions, when the yolk rotates in its small pool of thin white as the egg is turned, one coil is wound up and the other unwound. Turning the egg in the same direction every time will wind up one of the chalazae and unwind the other too far thus disrupting the structure and causing the death of the embryo.

The pool of thin white is restrained round the yolk by the rest of the thick white. This is also attached to the shell membranes at each end of the egg. Except at the end of the egg, where it is attached to these membranes, an outer layer of thin white immediately under the shell surrounds the thick white. The thin white also has structural functions. That part of the yolk adjacent to the germinal disc is less dense than the rest of the yolk, so it tends to float up when the egg is turned, thus rotating the yolk so that the germinal disc is always at the top.

The watery fluid permits this rotation. In the early stages of development of the embryo, before it has developed a blood system to bring nutrients and oxygen to it, the embryo can only use those nutrients that actually are in contact with it. Turning the egg gives it a new immediate source of food and oxygen within the thin white.

Dissolved gases diffuse much faster through water than through jelly. The outer layer of thin white is thus essential for the necessary exchange of carbon dioxide out, and of oxygen in, until the development of the embryonic membranes.

THE SHELL MEMBRANES AND AIR SPACE

There are two membranes around the egg, which are loosely adherent to each other. The outer one is firmly attached to the shell; indeed the shell is deposited on it. As the shell contents shrink with evaporation and utilisation by the embryo, the two membranes separate at the broad end of the egg to form an air space. This air space is vital for the development of the embryo. It allows evaporation within a rigid structure, pre-hatching movements, and the embryo to breathe. The size of the air space increases as incubation proceeds. Monitoring its size is a vital part of the management of incubation.

THE SHELL

Egg-shaped is mathematically described as an irregular ovoid, because one end is broader and flatter than the other, and the maximum diameter is nearer the broader end. This really means that if an egg is rolled along a flat surface, it will roll in a circle. Those birds that nest in tree cavities tend to produce nearly spherical eggs, while those such a gulls, that nest on narrow ledges, have markedly pointed ones, that will roll in a circle if disturbed.

A Fresh Egg

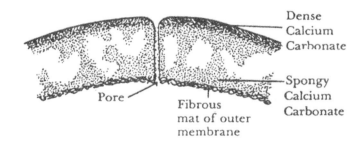

Dense Calcium Carbonate

Spongy Calcium Carbonate

Pore

Fibrous mat of outer membrane

B After Hatching

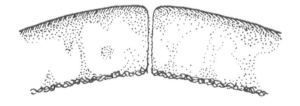

The dense outer layer of calcium carbonate remains, but the inner spongy layer has been absorbed by the embryo

Fig.1.2. Microscopic section through a shell

The largest and strongest mechanical structure that can be made from a given amount of material is a hollow sphere or ball.

The outside of the sphere is a thin layer of very dense material, and inside this is a slightly thicker layer arranged like a sponge. The eggshell is so constructed. It takes considerable force to crush an intact egg from the outside, but very little force to poke a hole in it from the inside, as the chick does at hatching time.

Many tiny holes or pores perforate the entire thickness of the shell. There are many more pores per square millimetre at the blunt end of the egg than elsewhere. The function of these pores is to permit the exchange of respiratory gases, carbon dioxide and oxygen, and to control the rate of evaporation of water. Infective bacteria can enter through these pores, though the structure keeps most of them out. The greatest number can enter if the shell is wet and dirty, and they are often in sufficient numbers to overcome the defence mechanisms of the membranes and albumen, and so produce an addled egg.

The porosity of the shell varies markedly from bird to bird. Ducks that lay in vegetation over water, or on damp marshy ground, tend to have very porous shells, whilst those birds that nest in rock cavities, or other dry situations, have very impermeable shells to prevent excessive evaporation of water.

Experiments carried out on Roulroul partridge housed in a humid tropical house produced normal eggs, but when the same hens were placed in a dryer house they produced thicker shelled eggs to prevent moisture loss. The granular inner layer of the shell is the store of calcium needed to form the bony structure of the embryo.

Chapter 2

FORMATION OF THE EGG

THE OVARY

The ovary is situated high in the abdominal cavity, attached to the spine and adjacent rib bones. Most animals have a pair of ovaries, but in birds one is usually rudimentary. In most species it is the left ovary that is functional. Occasionally, the right ovary begins to function. This, being a rudimentary organ, has elements of both male and female, so that it functions as an ovotestis, producing both male and female hormones. When this happens, the bird appears to change sex, either partially or completely. It is, however, always sterile.

If a bird has its ovary removed surgically, or destroyed by disease, its ovotestis functions and the hen will develop the gaudy plumage of the cock at the next moult. Such sex changes have been reported quite commonly in exotic ducks, particularly in Carolinas and Falcated Teal. They have also been noted quite frequently in pheasant hens if they reach a ripe old age. This female plumage changing process is known as gynandry, from the Greek (a masculine woman).

Fig. 2.1 A gynandrous Golden pheasant

STIMULATION TO FUNCTION

In the non-breeding season the ovary is a small wrinkled organ, about the size of a nut, but it enlarges at the breeding time to produce the germinal cells, each microscopic, but enclosed with an enormous supply of fat and protein in a delicate sac - the yolk. They are released one at a time into the oviduct. The release of two will give a double-yolked egg.

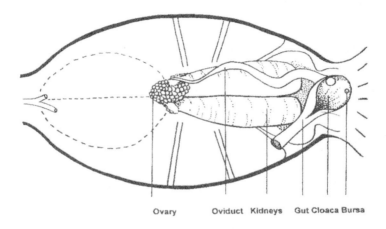

Ovary   Oviduct Kidneys   Gut Cloaca Bursa

Fig. 2.2 Female duck in non-breeding condition

Light

The ovary is stimulated to function in the spring by a variety of factors, the chief of these being an increase in the hours of daylight, or, more accurately, a decrease in the hours of darkness.

The intensity of the light is not critical, but the duration is important. The receptor for this light stimulus is obviously the eye, but the entire head area is also sensitive, as completely blind birds still come into lay. It has been found that if blind birds had hoods placed over their heads, they do not come into lay.

Temperature

The second most important factor is temperature: a cold spring means a late hatching season.

In near-arctic places, such as Iceland, the weather can influence the breeding season by as much as three weeks in those birds that are resident there, such as the Barrow's Goldeneye, Scaup, Redbreasted Merganser, Longtail and Scaup.

However, those birds that migrate enormous distances to breed in the Arctic, such as Barnacle, Brent and Snow Geese, have a deadline to get their young fully grown and flying before the onset of winter, so they are not nearly so temperature sensitive, and come into lay by the calendar, whatever the weather.

Pheasants are particular influenced by the weather, a cold wet spring often being the harbinger of a bad breeding season. Even the domestic hen which, by selective breeding, lays all the year round, will not lay well when the temperature drops below 15.5°C (60°F), or if there are less than eight hours of daylight.

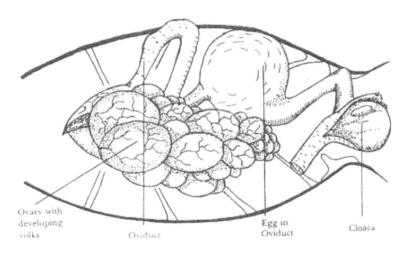

Ovary with
developing
yolks

Oviduct

Egg in
Oviduct

Cloaca

Fig. 2.3. Female duck in breeding condition

Territory and courtship rituals

The third most important factor is psychological. The commercial laying hen will perform very happily in a wire cage all on its own, but most wild birds need the additional stimulation of the presence of a sexually active male, and a firm pair bond. They need space and peace for their courtship rituals, and a firm territory to defend and nest in. Overcrowded birds, paddling about in the mud, will not breed. These territorial requirements vary enormously. A pair of geese mated for life, stakes out a well-defended area in which to nest and will tolerate no other bird within it. With the exception of the Lesser Whitefront who guards his goose from as far as fifty metres away, all ganders stay in the vicinity of the nest, aggressively defensive. The only thing on which they will launch an unprovoked attack is another female wandering around. Her gander will not come to her defence, being preoccupied with his territory and nest site.

Duck territories are not so well defined. The drake must have an area of shoreline or bank to defend from others of his own species, the duck nesting anywhere within hundreds of metres of it.

Cock game pheasants establish a large, loose area, and invite as many hens as they can to nest in it, but they do flock mate provided that the cocks can get away from one another. It is usual to run a ratio of one cock to six hens, as opposed to the domestic cockerel, which can happily look after fifteen to twenty.

French or Red-legged partridge will flock mate on a one-to-one basis, each pair co-existing with the others, but the English or Grey partridge pair needs to be alone. The cocks will fight to death if confined together, and so will most of the ornamental pheasants.

Many of the grouse family have traditional display areas, where the cocks gather together to lek. There is little fighting; the birds try to out-display each other, the winners getting the best sites. The hens then mate with the cocks of their choice, usually the dominant ones, and then disappear to nest kilometres away.

Hormonal mechanisms

The increase in light duration, and sexual excitement acts directly on the bird's brain. At the base of the brain is a small gland, the pituitary. The nervous stimulation causes this to make and release into the blood a series of hormones cyclically produced and released.

1.   Follicle stimulating hormone (FSH). The presence of this FSH stimulates the ovary to enlarge, and to form egg yolks. It also causes the ovary to secrete oestrogen, the female hormone, that makes the rest of the female genital tract - the oviduct - enlarge and become functional.

2.   Luteinising hormone (LH). This causes the egg follicles to mature and release the egg yolk from the ovary. It also stimulates the ovary to produce progesterone, which causes the oviduct to secrete the albumen and the shell, which are then added to the yolk, as this passes down the oviduct to the outside world. In addition, LH also raises the level of calcium, phosphorus, proteins, and certain vitamins in the blood, so that these become available to the developing egg.

3.   Prolactin. This hormone is released after the bird has laid a clutch of eggs, and causes it to go broody.

DIAGRAMMATIC FORMATION OF THE YOLK
(see opposite)

A.   *The primordial follicle appears on the surface of the ovary.*

B.C.D.   *Increasing deposits of fat and protein within the cell to form the yolk.*

E.   *The follicle containing the yolk ruptures, releasing the yolk into the abdominal cavity; from there it enters the infundibulum of the oviduct. Sperms, from a prior mating, wait in the folds of the upper oviduct to fertilise the egg. Although only one yolk is shown, many at various stages of development are forming simultaneously. The ruptured follicle shrinks to become another scar on the surface of the ovary.*

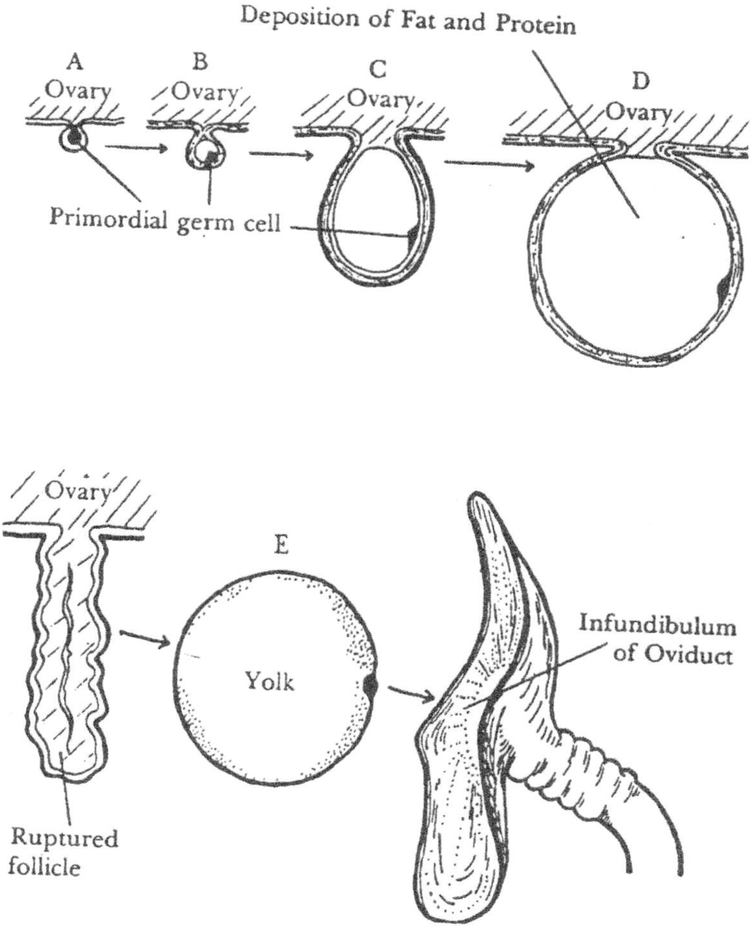

Fig.2.4. Diagrammatic formation of the yolk

THE OVIDUCT

Most of the females in the animal kingdom have a single uterus, or womb, with a fallopian tube leading to the ovaries on each side. In birds, not only is the right ovary absent, but so is the right fallopian tube. The left one is continuous with the uterus, and forms the oviduct. This is a hollow tube that embraces the ovary at one end, and opens into cloaca or vent at the other.

In the non-breeding season, it is a thin pencil-like tube, but as it comes into function, it lengthens and folds into two or more loops, and grows in diameter to accommodate the egg.

Fertilisation

After the egg cell is released from the ovary with the yolk, it is fertilised at the top of the oviduct by sperm, which has travelled up from the cloaca. Fertilisation cannot take place once the yolk has started its journey down the oviduct. Sperm can remain viable and fertilise successive eggs after a single mating for up to one week in pheasants, guinea fowl and chickens, two weeks in ducks, and three weeks in turkeys. The passage of the yolk down the oviduct takes about twenty-four hours.

During this time, the fused egg germinal cell and sperm begin to develop and form a mass of cells by division into two, four, eight, sixteen, and so on, until by the time of laying this can be seen as a small white spot, about 4mm in diameter, on the yolk. Further development is arrested by the cooling of the laid egg, but resumed on incubation. Slow development continues at temperatures over 21.1°C (70°F) but if this is prolonged for any length of time, it can weaken the germ fatally. A non-fertilised egg still develops a similar white spot, but no further development ever takes place.

The temperature inside the hen is 41.6°C (107°F), which is far too high for successful incubation. Some strains of domestic hen are known to take much longer than twenty-four hours to form an egg, and their apparent fertility is very low. The eggs were fertilised, but the germ died of overheating before the egg was laid. It is possible that many apparently infertile eggs are really very early deaths.

14

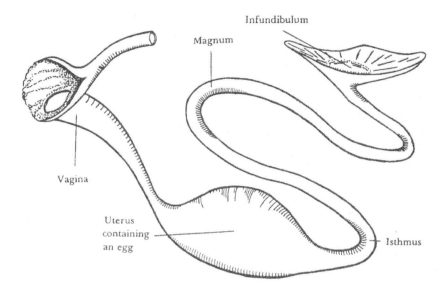

Fig. 2.5. Diagram of an oviduct

Deposition of the albumen
    In the upper part of the oviduct the four layers of albumen are deposited in order. First the chalciferous layer of fairly dense albumen in a thin membrane round the yolk; then a layer of thin, watery albumen; next, the thick white with twisted strands that form the suspensory ligament of the yolk, the chalazae. Finally, the outer coat of thin albumen is added.

Deposition of membranes and shell
    The membranes are added in the middle portion of the oviduct. Two separate layers are added, the outer one of which is the ground matrix on to which the calcium carbonate of the shell is deposited in the lowest portion of the oviduct, the uterus, or shell gland.
    Electron microscopy shows that the protein fibres of the membranes are woven into a mat, fairly loose on the inside and much denser on the outside. The chalky calcium carbonate is deposited in a loose granular structure on the inside, and the embryo uses this to form its bones; the outer shell is much denser and

stronger, its main function being protection.

There is considerable species variation in the pigments added to the shell for camouflage, and in the thickness and porosity of the shell, as well as in the texture and thickness of a waxy cuticle on the surface of the egg.

The egg is finally expelled by contraction of the shell gland. Stress or disease can cause the premature expulsion of a soft-shelled egg.

Chapter 3

PRODUCTION OF SPERM BY THE MALE

ANATOMY OF THE REPRODUCTIVE ORGANS

Unlike the female, which has only one ovary, both testes are present in the male. They occupy a similar anatomical site as the ovaries, high in the back wall, adjacent to the anterior end of the kidneys. The testes of the domestic cockerel are permanently enlarged, for he is in breeding condition for most of his adult life, but in all other birds there is a marked seasonal variation in their size. In the non-breeding season, they are small, insignificant organs, but at the height of sexual activity, they can enlarge to ten times their resting size.

Microscopically, the testes consist of a mass of convoluted tubules, rather like a jumble of pieces of string cobbled up into a ball. The cells lining the tubules produce sperm, and the cells between the tubules (interstitial cells) produce the male hormones.

Each of these string-like tubules ends in a common duct, the vas deferens, which conveys the sperm down to the penis and cloaca.

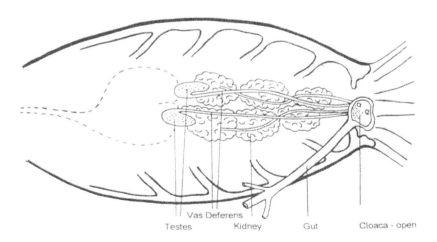

Fig. 3.1. Reproductive organs of a young male partridge

17

Certain species of birds, such as the ratites (Rheas, Ostriches, etc.) and waterfowl, have developed an erectile copulatory organ, the penis, but in all the others this is much less well developed.

VENT SEXING
Due to the presence of this male copulatory organ, it is possible to distinguish the sexes at times when there is no other difference in plumage, size or behaviour. Most of the commercial poultry produced today are sexed at the time of hatching for economic reasons.

Sexing day old chicks is a very skilled operation, and the birds must be handled gently for damage can easily be done to the delicate organs. Professional chicken sexers can handle about a thousand chicks per hour, with virtually 100% accuracy. The faeces are removed from the intestines by gentle pressure on the abdomen, and the cloaca then everted so that the sexual organ can be inspected.

In chickens and pheasants there are subtle, but positive, differences in the sexes that can be detected by a skilled sexer. Day old ducks and geese are much easier, as the male organ is plainly visible like a small bean shoot. During adolescence it is not so prominent, but very obvious in an adult

DNA SEXING
During recent years, an additional method of sexing rare and exotic species has been developed by the use of DNA analysis of samples taken from a specimen. After the chick has hatched, if the membrane left within an egg is taken and analysed in a laboratory, the sex of the chick from this eggshell can be accurately determined.

In the case of older birds, a blood feather taken from the wing or a few feathers taken from the breast can also be used to determine the sex of a bird, but in all cases an accepted marker sample of known origin must be available for comparison. Those laboratories undertaking such work have established a large data bank of markers for reference. DNA sexing is too costly an operation to be used for large numbers, as in the case of a large hatchery, but is a great asset when endangered species are involved.

STIMULATION OF THE SEXUAL ORGANS TO FUNCTION

Light
The prime stimulus to sexual function in the male is light, as in the female. The important factor is the decreasing number of hours of darkness, not the intensity of light during the day. In many species of birds it takes longer for the male to respond to the light stimulus than the female. This can result in clear or infertile eggs at the start of the breeding season. All species of birds that normally only reproduce in the spring can be induced to breed out of season by subjecting them to artificial light cycles. It is usual, under these conditions, to segregate the males, and start the increasing light cycle two to three weeks earlier than for the females, in order to ensure good fertility.

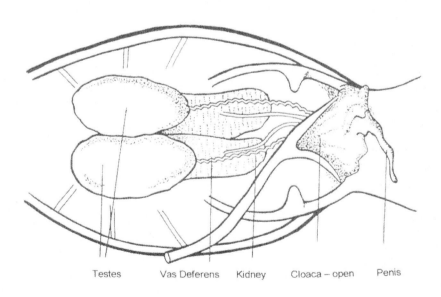

Testes   Vas Deferens   Kidney   Cloaca – open   Penis

Fig. 3.2. Reproductive organs of a male mallard in breeding
condition

Temperature
The males are just as sensitive to temperature as the females, sexual activity being markedly decreased under about 15.5°C (60°F). Very hot weather has an equally depressing effect. Secondary sexual organs, such as the wattles and comb, can be damaged by frost. Severe damage or illness can so affect the bird that it loses all interest in sexual behaviour, and goes out of breeding condition rapidly.

Climatic conditions
Certain waterfowl that live in arid semi-tropical areas, such as the Australian Mane goose and various members of the tree duck family, only come into breeding condition in response to periods of rain and abundant water, because there would not otherwise be food for the young. Since these wet periods come erratically, the breeding periods of the birds are unpredictable. Black swans, Cape Barren geese, Australian Shellduck and certain other birds respond to the shortening day, as this heralds the rainy season in their natural habitat.

Environment
Overcrowded birds paddling about in mud will not breed. Bad housing, dirty conditions, poor drinking water, and inadequate feeding will all depress the sexual activity of the male. In marginally bad conditions the female will sometimes lay a few eggs, but these are usually infertile.

HORMONAL MECHANISMS
The mechanisms of sexual development are similar to those of the female. Increasing light and temperature act directly on the brain. The pituitary gland, at the base of the brain, releases two hormones that cause the testicles to enlarge and function.

1.   Follicle stimulating hormone (FSH). This is identical with the female FSH, and causes the testicles to grow larger, and the cells lining the testicular tubules to start developing to produce sperm. It also promotes the growth of the interstitial cells between the tubules.

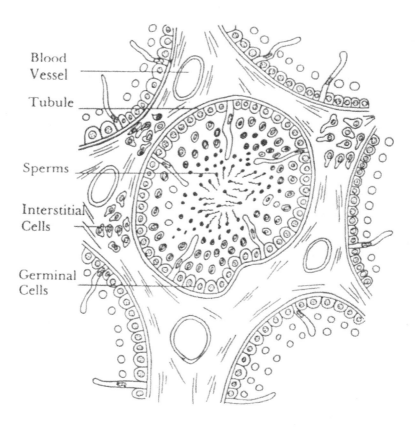

Blood
Vessel

Tubule

Sperms

Interstitial
Cells

Germinal
Cells

Fig. 3.3. Microscopic section of a functional testis

2.   **Interstitial cell stimulating hormone** (ICSH). This is probably identical to the female luteinising hormone, and causes the tubule cells to ripen into spermatozoa, and interstitial cells to start producing testosterone, the male hormone.

In some species, the male shares in the duties of incubation and in most the male guards the female and the nesting site. It is possible that prolactin, or a similar substance, is responsible for this change in behaviour.

Testosterone
This hormone, produced in the testicles of males in virtually the entire animal kingdom in response to stimulation from the brain and pituitary gland, is responsible for the development of the secondary sexual characteristics, be these the hair on the chin of an adolescent, the mane of a lion, or the bloom on the plumage of a healthy bird that denotes breeding condition.

It also causes the bird to become more dominant and aggressive, and to indulge in breeding displays as well as copulation, besides stimulating the tubules to produce and release the spermatozoa.

The development of secondary sexual characteristics and breeding condition
A bird deprived of its sexual organs will develop the plumage of the cock, though the colours will be muted, and it will have poorly developed wattles, comb, etc. It is positive secretion of oestrogens that give the females their plumage. The first feathers of young birds are very poorly sex differentiated, and the low levels of sex hormones in adolescence and in the non-breeding season are sufficient to cause the normal development. Increased output of testosterone puts a bloom on the feathers and enlarges the display organs. The knob on the bill of male Shelduck grows and glows with colour, as do the facial wattles of the pheasants.

Birds that moult into an eclipse plumage at the end of the breeding season do so in response to a dramatic drop in testosterone levels, combined with other hormonal changes. The dowdy female-type plumage helps to protect them from predators while they skulk flightless in the undergrowth, but some traces of masculinity remain in the feathers.

Territory and pre-copulatory displays
It appears to be an essential prerequisite to successful fertilisation in most species, that the male works himself up to it by a series of displays, and by successfully defending a chosen territory. All species have certain behaviour patterns in common, but the displays vary from the gaudy tail erection of the peacock to the furtive burp whistling of the common teal, via the grotesque contortions of the grouse family. Perhaps the success of the mallard as a species is due to the fact that its courtship is predominantly rape.

USE OF ADMINISTERED HORMONES

It is possible to increase the aggressiveness and sexual activity of a disappointing but valuable male by administering testosterone in small weekly injections, but this will work only if the bird is otherwise healthy, and has normal pituitary function. Poor pituitary function due to disease, poor environment, bulling, etc. can be overcome with artificial hormone injections, but this is experimental and expensive. It is far better to restore function by improved management.

The sexual activity of a male bird treated with hormones may be significantly increased, but as he can only produce a limited quantity of spermatozoa in any breeding season, the fertility of eggs from the extra hens mated to him could be low.

Chapter 4

FERTILITY

An infertile egg has no chance of hatching; successful mating has not taken place. There is no genetic plan to form a new bird, so the egg is just an accumulation of food with no possible future. Infertility is usually the fault of the male, or in its management.

Infertility must be distinguished from poor hatchability. An egg can be infertile, but possess defects or deficiencies that prevent it from developing into a perfect chick. If, at the end of incubation, the broken-out egg looks as if it could be fried for breakfast, it was infertile. If it does not look like a fresh egg, it was fertile, but died at some stage of development. Even if the embryo died in the first few days or hours of incubation, the enzymes it had already formed before death will continue to act upon the yolk, and cause it to rot and liquify. Such an egg is a perfect culture medium for bacteria, which may then turn the egg contents into the smelly, addled mess that is only too familiar. This egg was not infertile.

Incubation results are usually expressed as a percentage of all the eggs set, or of fertile eggs set. It is important to distinguish between genuinely infertile eggs, and those that were fertile but came to an early demise.

FACTORS AFFECTING FERTILITY

Age

The age of the male has a very marked influence on fertility. Young birds, though sexually mature and giving the appearance of breeding condition, are often not sufficiently dominant to mate successfully and frequently. Even if mating does take place, the bird may not have produced sufficient semen to fertilise all the eggs in the clutch. It is a well-known fact that early hatched pheasants lay more eggs, of better fertility and hatchability, than their later hatched siblings.

Most geese do not lay until their third year. The occasional goose lays in her second year, but too often her gander of the same age has been unable to fertilise the eggs.

Nearly all pheasants and ducks, with notable exceptions, are fertile at one year old. The first eggs laid by chicken pullets are usually smaller than those laid later on, and their fertility is poor. For this reason, eggs laid during the first two or three weeks by poultry flocks are not set to hatch.

Fertility also declines with age. An old bird is not so vigorous as he should be, and the frequency of mating, and the number of sperms produced at each mating, gets less with the passage of time. Birds do not have a menopause and they attempt to breed right up to death, but in later years fertility is often poor.

Commercial chickens and ducks are not considered to be economic after their breeding season. Game pheasants are usually kept for one year only, but this is more to prevent the build-up of disease in the pens than because of the declining fertility. The cocks also develop excessively long spurs that can damage the hens at mating. These birds could go on for as long as four years, but it is usually only exotic species that are allowed to do so, where every egg is valuable.

As a general rule, ducks are good for four to seven years, and geese for ten to fifteen years. Ganders aged twenty-five have been known to produce fertile eggs. Some exotic species of pheasant, such as the Himalayan Monal and Crestless Fireback have been known to lay fertile eggs at 16 years or more. Many other exotic pheasants will lay fertile eggs for ten or more years.

Health

An obviously sick bird has no hope of breeding. However, birds that appear at a casual glance to be in perfect health, and in breeding condition, may have some underlying chronic disease that renders them infertile. Avian tuberculosis, aspergillosis, and coccidiosis are only too common in places where birds have been kept for years. Leukosis and microplasma adversely affect the victims. Birds that have apparently recovered from salmonella infections, or Newcastle disease, have poor fertility and equally bad hatchability.

Aged birds suffering from arthritis tend not to mate and any injury to feet or wings can prevent mating in an otherwise healthy bird.

Nutrition

Gross or marginal deficiencies in either the quantity or the quality of the food can have adverse effects on fertility. Where the deficiency is great, the hens do not lay eggs, nor do the cocks fertilise them. All too often there is sufficient food for eggs to be produced, but deficiencies in it give very poor fertility and even poorer hatchability. It seems strange that a hen can produce over a season almost her own body weight of eggs on such a diet, but the cock cannot produce the tiny quantity of sperm needed to fertilise them. A proportion of such eggs will be fertile. But the deficiencies within them will render them unhatchable.

Where the diet is not balanced, and there is too much starch and too little protein, the birds can become overweight. A bird, like some of the human race, can become too fat to bother.

Parasites

Internal parasites, such as nematodes, gapes, gizzard worm and acuria, are a very common cause of infertility. The physical presence of the worms can debilitate the bird by cutting down its food intake, but more commonly they cause secondary deficiencies of vitamins and other nutrients. All breeding birds should be wormed routinely.

External parasites, fleas, lice mites, etc, are a constant source of irritation to the birds, and can affect their health. The constant blood loss can render them anaemic. Concentrations of parasites round the vent can lead to feather pecking, and secondary infections in such wounds can render the bird sterile.

There are many proprietary brands of insecticide that are effective and harmless to the birds, and one should be used routinely before each breeding season.

Environment

Bored birds, up to their ankles in mud and pecking seven bells out of each other, do not lay fertile eggs. The basic rules of elementary stockmanship must apply to all captive creatures.

The housing should be adequate for the species of bird, be it chicken run, covered aviary, or open pond. They should be protected from extremes of temperature and rainfall, and have access to clean water at all times. Should the area degenerate into a sea of mud, rapid build-up of disease will occur.

Light and temperature stimulate breeding condition. Sometimes this is not synchronised in the male and the female.

Most waterfowl can only mate on water. Lack of a suitable

swimming area is a common cause of infertility.

Stress

Bad environment and/or bad management usually cause this. Enclosures which are too small or badly sited, so that the birds spend their time running fruitlessly up and down the wire trying to hide or escape is not conducive to good fertility. The constant presence of potential predators in threatening attitudes, such as children poking sticks through the wire, cats trying to get in, and dogs rushing up and down outside, will put a timid bird off. Vermin continually disturbing them will do the same, besides consuming all the food.

Bulling by other species of birds or the pressure of other males constantly trying to get in on the act can, and often does, prevent successful mating.

Unlike the mallard, whose courtship is predominantly rape, many species of birds need time and peace to undergo their stylised courtship rituals. If there is not a suitable area, or constant disturbance prevents it, mating will not take place.

Two or more males fighting for the same territory and display areas give very poor fertility. Conversely, if those species that need the stimulation of other males displaying to set them off are housed next to each other, where they can see but not interfere with the pen next door, each cock feels that he has won the encounter through the wire, and mates with his hen to prove it. This does not work with adjacently penned geese, as the instinct to clear his territory of rivals overcomes everything else, so a more substantial barrier, such as a hedge or solid fence must separate them.

Psychological castration

Where birds are flock mated, with several cocks looking after many more hens, a pecking order is established among the cocks, so that the dominant cock knocks another cock off a hen, and mates with her himself. The second dominant cock will do the same to any other cock, bar the top one, and so on down the line. The bottom bird of the pecking order may be so knocked about that he goes out of condition. If this bird is then separated and given hens of his own, he will still fail to mate. Psychologically, he has been castrated.

Preferential mating

In birds, such as Red-legged partridge, where the cock is quite capable of mating with several hens and has been put in a pen and expected to do so, he will often form a pair bond with one of the hens, and completely ignore the others who will then lay infertile eggs. This can occur even with the domestic hen, where certain birds, being so unattractive to the cock, fail to claim his attentions. In those species that are monogamous and form a strong pair bond, the cock will mate with only one hen.

Abnormal imprinting

In the first few hours after hatching, the chick attaches itself to the first thing it sees, identifying this as mother and following it wherever it goes. In the natural state this is, of course, the parent bird. Some birds, notably the goose family, imprint very firmly, and this lasts for life. Most, however, lose this imprinting as they grow and become independent. Where this imprinting has been particularly strong, such as hand-reared geese, they will only want to mate with another of the objects that reared them. If a clutch have been reared together, they will mate with each other, but single hand-reared birds are convinced that the person who reared them is the only possible mate, and are totally useless as a breeding birds. Some years ago, a well-known aviculturist successfully reared a solitary Red-breasted gander under an infra-red light, with only a food dish and an aluminium water pot for company. Flushed with success, he acquired, at vast expense, a female, and the two lived happily together. (In those days Red-breasted geese were very difficult to rear in captivity.) The female came into lay, but the gander wanted nothing to do with her, persistently driving her away from the aluminium water pot, to which he was devotedly mated. He called incessantly to this water pot, and got very frustrated trying to mount it. It was changed for an open trough, but the bird pined and went out of condition.

In desperation, the aviculturist brought another gander for his female. This one had been reared in a cowshed and was fixed on cattle; he instantly made for and wooed the brown milk cow in the same paddock. The brown cow was sold and replaced by a black one, but it made no difference; the gander didn't seem to notice the change.

Pheasants and ducks are not as extreme as this, but imprinting still takes place. Broods of mixed species grow up not knowing what they are, and regularly cross-mate with the species they have been reared with. This can be a difficult problem to cure.

The fashion in the 1970's was to rear rare and exotic pheasants singly in small, white-painted wooden boxes, with an overhead white light. This is very successful in preventing disease and feather pecking, but the birds can be imprinted negatively on nothing but white, brightly-lit surroundings.

Today, when using this method, most breeders use a dull emitter or a red coloured lamp to brood their chicks. On reaching adult life and full breeding potential, they are just not interested in the opposite sex: their breeding instinct has been stifled at birth. The only hope for such birds is artificial insemination. This problem does not appear to be evident today; perhaps in the 1970's most stock was very inbred, whereas today there have been inter-continental exchanges, plus new blood received from the wild, which allows viable chicks to be raised.

Happily, clutches of the same species reared artificially imprint on each other.

Inbreeding

Where excessive inbreeding has taken place, recessive traits come to the fore. The birds tend to be weaker, lack vigour, and have a poor display. Sexual interest is low, and the cocks produce small quantities of poor-quality semen. Some of these recessive traits are lethal, so that even if fertilisation takes place, the germ dies before development, giving every appearance of an infertile egg. This can be the fault of the hen, as well as of the cock.

New blood, or out-breeding to another strain, has the opposite effect – hybrid vigour – as neither bird has the same recessive traits, so the dominant aspects of both birds become apparent.

This phenomenon is utilised in the commercial broiler chicken production. Four pure grandparent strains are kept. Two of these strains are mated together to produce the parent hens, and the other two to produce the cocks. The hybrid vigour of the final cross gives the necessary strength and quality to the broiler chicken. Mating these broilers together will give chicks of poorer quality than the parents.

Primary sterility

It sometimes happens that a perfectly healthy cock, of impeccable parentage, does not produce any sperm at all. He has defects, either of the testicles or of the ducts leading from them.

There is usually no obvious cause for this, but it can be produced by several factors. Poor incubation technique, particularly overheating or fluctuating incubator temperatures, can adversely affect the reproductive organs as they are forming. Testicles so affected function poorly in adult life. The laying potential of the hen can be similarly curtailed.

Primary pituitary dysfunction can fail to stimulate the testes sufficiently to produce sperm. Viral infections can produce sterility. (This can also happen to young men who catch mumps.) Infection ascending the vas deferens from the cloaca can cause scarring that prevents the sperm being released at mating.

ARTIFICIAL AIDS TO FERTILITY

Where a species or strain is so inbred that it has lost the urge to mate, or, in the case of the domestic turkeys, where the conformation of the bird, to give the maximum meat in the right places, renders it anatomically impossible for them to mate naturally, the only answer is artificial insemination.

The technique is simple, but skilled. The birds are housed in small wire cages, and accustomed to being handled. A rigorous half-hour chase, prior to catching the bird, does not enhance the chances of a successful outcome.

Semen is obtained from the cock by holding the bird firmly by the legs with one hand, its breast resting on the forearm. Its back is stroked gently but firmly from head to tail with the other hand for a few minutes, and then the abdomen is stroked towards the vent. This will cause the emission of a few drops of semen, which an assistant immediately sucks up with a small pipette. The semen must be transferred at once to the oviduct of the hen. Depending on the quantity, more than one hen can be inseminated.

To inseminate the hen, she is held in a similar manner to the cock and the vent everted to show the oviduct. It is impossible to do this in a hen that is not laying eggs. If force is required, the hen is not ready and damage will be the only result. Having exposed the oviduct, the

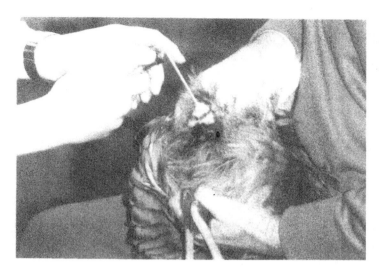

Fig. 4.1. Massaging a Brown-eared pheasant cock to obtain semen. Note the position of the handler, with the assistant poised to suck the precious ejaculate into a glass tube

Fig. 4.2. The vent of the hen everted to expose the oviduct

semen is placed directly within it by blowing down the pipette. Fertile eggs should result within two days.

Hormone injections have been used to bring the birds into prior breeding condition.

Where hatching eggs are required out of the normal breeding season, this can be achieved with artificial light cycles. Using the guinea fowl as an example, the day old birds are reared under continuous light for the first ten weeks. This stimulates them to eat more and grow faster. A minimum of ten hours light per day is essential for this period. After this the light is reduced to eight hours a day and kept at this level until the birds are twenty-two weeks old.

They are now transferred into cages, and each week the daily light is increased by half an hour until, at thirty-four weeks, the birds are on sixteen hours of light per day, and at maximum egg production. The intensity of the light is not critical, but too much will cause cannibalism. During this time, the temperature must not drop below 60°F (15.5°C).

They are run for a thirty-eight week production period, during which time each bird will have laid 170-180 eggs. The cock birds, if left with the hens, do not give good fertility, so it is customary to use artificial insemination every three days. Suitable modification of this technique can give fertile out-of-season eggs from most species of bird.

A decreasing light cycle is used extensively in large turkey production, for it delays the onset of sexual maturity and hence the birds get fatter and are more contented.

Under these artificial conditions, it can happen that the cocks do not come into breeding condition simultaneously with the hens. This can also be a common cause of infertility where birds are housed naturally. The only cure is to light up the cocks, commencing several weeks ahead of the hens.

Some cocks are just naturally infertile, and there is little that can be done about this, except to change them.

CHAPTER 5

HATCHABILITY

The fact that an egg is fertile does not guarantee that it will hatch. Although poor incubation takes its toll of far too many eggs each year, many eggs do not hatch under the best of conditions, for they possess defects or deficiencies that prevent them from doing so. Bad management can spoil a good quality egg, but a poor egg cannot be improved after it has been laid.

Hatchability is usually measured as the percentage of fertile eggs set that hatch, not the percentage of all eggs set.

If the egg is regarded as consisting of a plan, or set of genetic instructions, together with sufficient tools and building materials to make the new bird, any errors or omissions in the plan, the tools, or the materials, will render the egg unhatchable, even though most of the development may take place.

In the same way, deterioration of the egg contents, brought about by bad storage, infection, and poor incubation, can also render it unhatchable, even though when first laid it was fully capable of developing into a new bird.

The greatest mortality from such defective or damaged eggs occurs late in incubation. They are dead in shell.

FACTORS AFFECTING HATCHABILITY

The age of the parent stock
Like fertility, hatchability is markedly influenced by the age of the parents. The eggs from very young birds often hatch very poorly. Either the germs are weak or improperly matured, or the basic metabolism of the laying hen is insufficiently geared up to provide the developing egg with all the necessary vitamins, minerals, etc.

Game pheasants that are twelve months old when they commence laying, lay far more good quality eggs than their sisters who are only nine months old at the start of the laying season. It is far better to keep the early-hatched birds for breeding stock, than merely to keep back the late hatchers.

As a bird ages, too, there is a gentle decline in the ability to put into the eggs that vital genetic spark that ensures a healthy, viable chick. A long period of laying seems to exhaust the bird's capacity to transfer to the eggs the essential micro-nutrients, even when there is no deficiency of such items in the diet.

This decline with age obviously varies enormously from species to species, but can be a very individual characteristic of individual birds. As a rule, hens, ducks and pheasants are not kept commercially after their second year, but geese can go on for over ten or twelve years. Those species that do not sexually mature until their second or third years tend to have a longer useful reproductive life than those that lay in their first spring.

Inheritance

Some birds, kept under perfect conditions, consistently lay eggs that are fertile but hatch very poorly. The eggs are genetically defective. Many pairs of genes are involved, affecting both the metabolism of the hen and the physiology of the embryo. Such genes are usually recessive; that is, they do not produce effects in the normal bird, being masked by a more dominant trait. Inbreeding to unmask a desirable recessive trait, such as feather colour, egg laying capacity, or growth rate, will usually unmask many undesirable recessive traits as well. These can vary, from insufficient strength to hatch; inability to mobilise vital nutrients from the body, and transfer these to the egg; thus preventing any embryonic development at all.

In some rare species of birds in captivity, which of necessity have been grossly inbred, these recessive traits have become so pronounced that the species is in danger of extinction. Too close inbreeding has lost many superb strains of domestic birds.

The only hope for such defective inbred creatures is to outcross to another strain, which, though it might have developed its own genetic defects, will have defects different from the first strain. The masking of these traits by dominant genes from the other strain will give a renewed vigour to the offspring. Hopefully, some individuals will inherit none of the harmed genes, and so keep the species going. This hybrid vigour is utilised extensively in the poultry industry to produce both meat and eggs more economically.

Some strains of both birds and animals do not seem to carry such undesirable recessive traits and can be inbred indefinitely without apparent harm. The most obvious example of this is the Australian rabbit. All the countless millions of these rabbits are descended from an original importation of seven individuals. Presumably, any individual rabbit with such undesirable traits did not produce viable descendants, these being removed by a process of natural selection. Similar selective family inbreeding has occurred in the migratory geese that nest in the Arctic. They tend to return to the same area each year to nest, choosing a near relative as a mate. Over countless numbers of years, this has given rise to five definite races of Canada Geese and three of Brent Geese. It is not until they are physically transplanted that the races interbreed. The hybrid vigour of this intermingling could well account for some of the success of the feral Canada's in the British Isles and elsewhere.

Health and environment
The environment in which birds are kept plays a decisive role in their state of health. Good health is a prerequisite of good fertility and hatchability.

Accommodation: The area in which the birds are housed must be suitable for that species of bird, and take into account such factors as its natural habitat, the time of year, temperature, light intensity, and prevailing weather conditions. The birds must be comfortable and clean.

Light: Most birds are stimulated to commence breeding by a change in the daily light duration. Not only are the reproductive organs affected, but also the entire metabolism of the hen is changed to make available the necessary constituents of the egg from her own body. Inadequate or unsuitable light conditions can affect this change in metabolism, to the detriment of the egg.

Temperature: Extremes of temperature also affect egg production. As with unsuitable light, the effect may not be great enough to cut down the total number of eggs, but it may be enough to affect the hatchability of these eggs, as they are marginally deficient in certain essential components.

Weather: Any factor that affects the comfort of the bird can affect the hatchability of the eggs it lays. Cold, draughty pens, with no shelter from the elements, do not bring out the best in the birds.

Build up of disease: In the natural state, birds have no control over the emptying of their bowels. Where they spend the most time, there will be the biggest heap of droppings, be it in the duck's water or under the pheasant's perch. These droppings are a major health hazard. Firstly, they contain all the waste products of the bird's biochemistry that, if re-eaten, will require considerable expenditure of energy to remove again and, if consumed in sufficient quantity, can be positively poisonous. Secondly, and even more importantly, they contain bacteria and the eggs of parasitic worms.

Bacteria that are normally present in the gut of healthy birds become pathogenic if their numbers rise above that which the bird can cope with. This can happen explosively, leading to sudden death, but more commonly it leads to a state of chronic debility.

Most birds carry some internal parasites that do them no harm whatsoever. If they are constantly re-infected, the parasitic load builds up very rapidly. Their physical presence can cut down the food intake, but the major effect is to cause a secondary vitamin deficiency. Both dramatically affect hatchability.

Access to natural food and water: Despite the best endeavours of the poultry food industry, it is an undoubted fact that most species of ornamental birds produce eggs of better hatchability if they have access to natural foods, such as grass, insects and worms. Unfortunately, such access often leads to bacterial and parasitic build up over the area, so that it is better on the whole to keep them free of such troubles by housing them on dry sand or wire mesh, and bringing grass clippings, etc. to them.

SPECIFIC DISEASES

The hatchability from weak or diseased birds is poor. Birds that have apparently recovered from a disease can be affected by it and lay poor eggs. The most obvious example of this is where a bird has suffered from an infection of the genital tract, which, although it has healed completely, has left the genital tract scarred. This scarring will produce mis-shapen eggs. All too often the damage is not visible but the egg is defective. The usual cause is malabsorption of foods from the intestine.

Virus infections

The poultry industry is beset by a whole host of virus diseases, most of which have only been identified after they have caused major epidemics in intensively housed birds. New viruses are constantly being discovered. The main ones so far identified are Newcastle Disease, Infectious bronchitis, Lymphoid leucosis, Marek's disease, Gumboro disease, Avian encephalomyelitis, Fowl pox, and Duck plague.

The mortality from all these viral diseases is high, and the hatchability from recovered birds is poor. After recovery, some birds still carry the virus, which can be transmitted through the egg, and affect other eggs in the incubator. It is the very genuine fear of outbreaks of virus diseases in the over-intensive poultry industry, accidentally introduced by imported ornamental birds, that is responsible for the harsh quarantine laws of most countries.

Bacterial infections

Avian Tuberculosis. This is a chronic wasting disease, responsible for much infertility and poor hatchability. Fortunately, the causal mycobacterium is not transmitted within the egg, nor is it usually carried on the shell. It is contracted from infected droppings, and tends to affect older birds.

Salmonella infections. There are many strains of salmonella, ranging from that which causes typhoid in humans, to the one that is the scourge of poultry, *salmonella pullorum*. This has been a problem for years, and virtually any species of bird can be affected. The disease used to be known as BWD— bacillary white diarrhea. Not only can it cause a high mortality and chronic debility, but also carriers can transmit the disease both within the egg and on the shell. The hatch from such eggs is appallingly bad, and the mortality in the chicks that do hatch approaches 100%. It is spread rapidly within the incubator, on egg collecting baskets, chick boxes and brooders, and in the absence of adequate sterilisation of such equipment, can cause untold damage. One unidentified carrier in the collection can ruin a season's hatch.

Fowl cholera. This is occasionally responsible for epidemic deaths. Recovered birds lay poor eggs and generally show signs of a malabsorption syndrome.

Streptococcal and staphyllococcal infections. These are the usual infecting agents of wounds, and often cause inflammation in the joints, feet, and oviduct. Contamination of the eggshell can cause many late deaths, as it is spread rapidly round the incubator.

E. Coli infections. There are many strains of *E. Coli,* all of which are associated with droppings. Some are really virulent. Foul ground and dirty nests mean automatic infection of both birds and eggs. *E. Coli* are responsible for many disappointing hatches.

Micoplasma. This is a small bacterium, approximating to the viruses, that is transmitted with the egg. It tends to be endemic within a flock, and is sometimes responsible for poor hatches.

Protozoan infections
The main ones are varieties of coccidiosis and blackhead. Chronic endemic infections are responsible for generalised debility, anaemia through blood loss, and diminished food intake. The parasites are not transmitted through the incubator, but affected birds lay eggs that hatch badly.

Intestinal and other internal parasites
Parasitic infestation not only cuts down the food intake, but can also produce signs of actual vitamin deficiency in the adult birds, despite an adequate diet. This will naturally affect the hatchability of any eggs laid. There are several types of worms and flukes, but none of them is carried on or in the egg.
Their main effect on hatchability is by secondary vitamin deficiency.

Fungal infections
Aspergillus, a mould found on damp and rotting vegetation, can attack most species of birds, usually in the lungs. It is a chronic wasting disease, almost always the terminal event in a bird debili-

tated from other causes, but it can cause epidemics in young birds. It is of paramount importance in incubation, as the spores can enter the egg both before and during incubation, and cause the contents to rot and explode. Transmission from egg to egg in the incubator is rapid and fatal.

DRUGS AND FOOD ADDITIVES
Many drugs given to laying birds can be detected in the eggs, sometimes for a considerable period after administration. Coccidiostats, antibiotics, and anthelmintics are added routinely to some poultry rations in low doses as a preventative, besides being used in higher concentrations therapeutically.

Any, or all, of these additives can lower the hatchability significantly, particularly if used in high doses. They act by interfering with the biochemical processes of the developing embryo, causing either death or deformity. Such drugs are said to be terratogenic. The action of thalidomide on the human embryo is a typical example of terratogenicity.

Some vitamins, notably folic acid, are manufactured by bacteria in the gut and the normal source of these is from such bacteria. Antibiotics kill these bacteria, and so cause a secondary deficiency of folic acid. Antibiotics should not be given to breeding birds, unless as treatment for a specific infection.

NUTRITION OF THE PARENT BIRDS
Nothing can be added to an egg once it has been laid. In order to develop successfully, the embryo must have everything needed for this process included within the shell. It is like a space ship, on a long, lone voyage of incubation.

Any deficiency in the hen's diet, or any disease or defect that prevents her transferring vital ingredients to the egg, will cause defects in the growth of the embryo and may cause its death.

The constituents of an egg are water, protein, fat, and minute traces of vitamins and minerals, and these must all come from the maternal diet.

Apart from the obvious case, where the confined birds are not given enough food for their daily needs, secondary deficiencies can be caused by such factors as overcrowding at the food troughs, bullying by other birds, insufficient water, internal parasites, and continual stress.

The essential components are carbohydrates, protein, fats, vitamins, minerals, roughage, grits and, of course, water. Not only must these be available in sufficient quantity but also the proportions of each must be correct.

Carbohydrates

The source of carbohydrate in the diet is predominantly starch from cereals, such as wheat, maize, oats and barley. Its function is to provide energy: energy for movement, growth, and the complicated biochemical processes of putting the necessary ingredients into the egg.

Chemically, carbohydrates are based on simple sugar molecules. These sugar molecules are joined in chains to form starches, which do not dissolve in water, and hence are easier for the plant to store.

More complex arrangements of sugar molecules form the cellulose and lignins, vital structural components of all plants that give them their rigidity. These celluloses and lignin's are classed in the diet as fibre.

It requires little chemical energy to split starches into their component sugars, and all birds can do this readily in the gut. However, they are unable to split the lignins and celluloses, and these have no energy value at all.

Simple sugars are easily broken down into smaller molecules, producing chemical energy for other reactions in the process. These smaller molecules are the building blocks making the chains of fatty acids, which combine to form storage fats. Weight for weight, fats provide much more energy than starches. 10% of an egg is fat; there is virtually no free carbohydrate stored within

This energy must come from the hen's diet, and birds usually eat to satisfy their energy requirements. The proportion of starch to fibre varies enormously among the different cereals. Since they are both chemically carbohydrates, but since the bird is only capable of utilising the energy contained within the starch, the carbohydrate content of a food is not measured by weight alone, but by the number of calories biologically available per unit of weight. As the diet will also contain some fats and oils, which are high in energy, these are also included in the energy content of a ration.

Proteins

Protein is the stuff of life. All flesh is made of protein. An egg is nearly 15% protein, most of which will be utilised to form the structure of the developing chick.

Dietary protein comes from both plant and animal sources. Wheat, soya, and grass are rich in protein, but maize, fruits, and vegetables are low. Fish meal, meat, bone, and feathermeal are all good sources of protein, as is incidental live food. Proteins are built up of chains of amino acids. The chains are woven into complex structures to form virtually all the tissues of the body, blood, muscles, bones, feathers, and skin.

Amino acids are all based on the ammonia molecule, NH_3, one of the three hydrogen ions of the basic ammonia molecule being replaced by a complex organic radicle. About twenty amino acids are known in nature, and all occur in some type of protein, the nature of the protein depending on the arrangement of the amino acids in the chains, and the way in which the chains are woven or linked together. Some amino acids are said to be nonessential; that is, the bird can manufacture them itself from other amino acids in the diet. Others are essential; that is, they cannot be manufactured by the bird, but must be ingested in the diet. Essential or non-essential, amino acids cannot be stored in the body, so that there must be a regular daily intake. Excess amino acids from protein in the diet are broken down to provide energy, and the NH_2 radicle excreted by the kidneys, after it has been detoxified to the inert uric acid. Where gross excesses of protein are fed, this uric acid accumulates in the body, and is deposited as a white film over most of the body's inner surfaces, causing visceral gout. In some instances, crystals of it appear in the joints, giving the more usual gout.

Food protein sources vary in their quality, not only depending on the proportions of essential and non-essential amino acids within them, but in the manner that the amino acids are linked together, and whether the bird possesses the necessary digestive enzymes to split them up. An old leather boot is an absolute goldmine of essential amino acids, but due to the chemical processes that turned the original skin into leather, the amino acids are so tightly bound together that, as an item of diet, it is useless.

Plant protein has entirely different amino acid proportions from animal protein and, fed on its own, can give rise to relative deficiencies of one or more essential amino acids.

For birds, the essential amino acids appear to be lysine, cystine, methionine, threonine, and tryptophan. The bird from others that are present in excess can readily manufacture all the rest.

Where the essentials are deficient in a diet made up purely from plant protein, they can be added either by including a proportion of good quality animal protein, or by adding synthetic purified chemicals to the ration in the exact amounts. In bulk commercial rations, day-to-day cost of the ingredients is the deciding factor in which method is used.

The quality of a ration is usually expressed as percentage protein, in units of available nitrogen, complete with the percentages of lysine, and methionine with cystine. Most breeder rations have 15-20% protein.

Most of the protein in an egg is found in the albumen. It consists of all the amino acids, in exactly the correct proportions, all loosely bound in simple chains, with few bonds between the chains. It is totally biologically available to the embryo, with virtually no waste. All these amino acids must be present in the hen's diet, and in the correct proportions, and biologically available to her. The quality of the protein is of far greater importance than the gross quantity.

Fats

Fats are an essential part of a bird's diet, usually constituting about 3% of it. The source is usually vegetable and fish oils, with waxes from fruit and insects, and some animal fat.

The fats have two functions, the visible and invisible; the visible being the storage of energy as body fat, and the invisible being vital structural components of tissues, particularly the brain, spinal cord, nerves, and blood vessels.

Storage fats are esters of fatty acid chains with glycerol. The fatty acids are long chains of carbon and hydrogen atoms. Those chains including the maximum number of hydrogen atoms are said to be saturated, and produce fats that are solid at body temperature. Those that contain considerably less than the maximum number of hydrogen atoms are said to be unsaturated, and the fats are liquid at body temperature. Storage fats produced from dietary carbohydrate tend to be mainly saturated. A proportion of dietary fat needs to be unsaturated or abnormal deposition of fats occurs in the body leading to artery troubles, heart attacks, etc. Structural fats are a multitude of complex molecules, involving cholesterols, lecithins, lipoproteins, and many others. At least two fatty acids are known to be essential for their formation in the body, linoic acid and linolenic acid. Birds are unable to synthesise these fatty acids, so they must be included in the diet. They occur widely in both plant and animal foods, but in much greater quantities in the latter. There are probably many more essential fatty acids occurring naturally that have not been positively identified as being essential for the chicken. It does not automatically follow that all species of birds need the same essential fatty acids.

As a general rule, herbivorous animals are capable of synthesising their own fatty acids, i.e. they are not essential, whereas carnivorous animals cannot make them, and must eat them in the diet, i.e. they are essential to them. It is quite possible that there is similar variation of capabilities of fatty acid synthesis in the bird world, and that some fatty acids are essential to some species.

Deficiency of essential fatty acids in the chicken causes failure to thrive, possible nervous disorders, and premature hardening of the arteries. This premature hardening of the arteries, with associated heart disorders, is a problem in certain tropical birds kept in confinement. The answer to this problem could lie in as yet unidentified essential fatty acids, present in their natural food but not present in commercial chicken rations.

Vitamins

Vitamins are essential to life. Although only present in the diet in minute amounts, absence of these substances from the food rapidly causes ill health and, ultimately, death. They cannot be manufactured in the body.

All of life's complicated biochemical processes are achieved by the action of enzymes. Each step in every process has its own specific enzyme which causes that reaction and no other. Thousands of enzymes are known, but many more thousands have yet to be identified. Each one is different. It would appear that each vitamin is an integral structural part of some enzyme or enzyme system.

Absence of that vitamin will thus not allow that particular step to proceed, be it a step in the breakdown of starch, the build up of

43

protein, or the excretion of waste products.

Deficiency of a vitamin in a ration can be total, partial, or merely marginal. The same diet that is quite adequate for a bird in the non-laying period can be deficient when that bird comes into lay, as the requirement of vitamins is greatly increased by the egg laying process. Since, to successfully hatch, each egg must contain all the vitamins needed for the formation and growth of the chick, extra vitamin is needed in the diet over and above that needed merely to produce an egg.

A ration may have more than enough vitamins in it to keep laying hens active, productive and healthy, but these eggs could hatch poorly as they are marginally deficient in one or more vitamins.

The early growth of the hatched chick is also dependent on the adequacy of vitamins in the hen's diet. Newly hatched chicks absorb vitamins from their food poorly, so need an adequate carry over from the egg.

Historical discovery of vitamins

When the presence of, and need for, vitamins was first suspected, it soon became apparent that there was more than one substance involved. As each substance was categorised, but not chemically identified, it was labelled with a letter of the alphabet: thus, Vitamins A, B, C, D and so on up to Vitamin K. By the time K was discovered, Vitamin B had been sub-divided into twelve different substances, some of which were identical with lettered vitamins, and some proved not to be vitamins at all. Most vitamins are now known by their chemical names, but for convenience the old classification is still used.

Vitamins A, D, E and K are fat soluble; they can be stored in the body fat. The B group and vitamin C are only soluble in water, and so cannot be stored in the body tissues. Birds must have a regular daily intake.

Vitamin A

Vitamin A is found only in animal tissues. The usual source is fish liver oils. It is not present in plants, but all green vegetables contain carotene pigments which birds can convert into Vitamin A. Synthetic Vitamin A is often used in commercial rations.

It is a very unstable, delicate substance, rapidly destroyed by light, heat, and exposure to air. Gross deficiency in adult birds causes blindness and rapid loss of condition. Marginal deficiencies are a common cause of poor hatchability, usually associated with stale food or lack of green stuff.

Vitamin D

Vitamin D is found in all animal tissues, but the usual source is fish liver oils. Ultraviolet light can convert certain sterols in the skin to Vitamin D, so that plenty of sunshine lessens the need for it. Winter sunshine or light through glass is not effective.

It is involved in the metabolism of calcium and phosphorus. Deficiency causes rickets: the bones are soft, so that they bend and deform, and the shell structure of the egg is abnormal. Marginal deficiency within the egg prevents the embryo mobilising the calcium of the shell, giving a very high dead in shell rate. Too much calcium in the diet, with insufficient phosphorus, increases the need for Vitamin D.

This can produce a relative deficiency, in spite of theoretically adequate amounts in the diet.

Vitamin E

The source of this vitamin is wheat germ oil, so that deficiencies only arise in birds that are fed on a mainly maize ration. This can produce poor hatches of chicks that don't thrive, and in extreme cases, exhibit crazy chick disease.

Vitamin K

This is found in all green leaves. It is an essential factor in the blood clotting mechanism. Deficiencies produce bleeding. It is only rarely deficient in eggs.

The B Group of vitamins

These are water soluble, and marginal deficiencies are a common cause of poor hatches.

B1 Thiamine. This is found in the husk and germ of all cereals, so deficiency is rare in poultry. Prisoners of war of the Japanese suffered terribly from lack of this vitamin, being fed only on polished rice.

B2 Riboflavin. This is the most important vitamin in incubation. Very large quantities are found in egg white, and deficiencies in hatching eggs are exceedingly common. It is widespread throughout nature, yeast and grass being good sources, but it is usually added to the ration as the pure synthetic compound. Deficiency causes a terrible hatch, with curly toe paralysis in the survivors. Marginal deficiencies give the characteristic clubbed down.

It is also manufactured by many bacteria, particularly in the rumen of cud-chewing animals, and by the bacteria of deep litter houses. Birds in deep litter houses can get by with less in the diet than can their sisters in battery cages.

Due to the high concentration needed in hatching eggs, there may be sufficient in the food for high egg production, but not enough for the eggs to hatch.

Nicotinic Acid, Niacin. This is the anti-pellagra vitamin for man. It is found in most plants except maize. A high maize diet can give a deficiency. The essential amino acid, tryptophan, can be converted to nicotinic acid, so that the presence of high quality protein renders it unnecessary. There is a large amount of tryptophan in eggs, so that poor quality protein can cause a secondary deficiency of this vitamin in hatching eggs.

B6. Pyridoxine. This is a very important vitamin for hatchability and early growth of the chick. It is concerned in the breakdown and synthesis of proteins, and is widespread in nature. Gross deficiencies are rare, but marginal deficiencies are common, and cause many dead in shell. A high protein diet increases the demand for pyridoxine, and so can cause a secondary deficiency in both the egg and the growing chick. When combined with a relative deficiency of manganese, lack of pyrodxine causes porosis. This is a softening of the growing bones, so that the large tendon of the hock joint can slip off the joint, and deform the leg.

Biotin and Pantothenic Acid. Deficiencies of both these vitamins are very rare in birds.

Fig 5.1 *A chick showing the results of inadequate feeding. This pathetic little creature is a bantam chick. Its parents were fed on wheat and scraps only. They laid well but the eggs hatched very badly. Note the poor posture and weakness of legs and feet.*

Fig 5.2 *The classical clubbed down of riboflavin deficiency.*

Folic Acid. This is an essential vitamin in the formation of red blood cells. Deficiency is rare, as it is synthesised by the normal bacteria of the gut. Problems only arise after the birds have been treated with antibiotics, which kill these bacteria. This can rapidly produce a deficiency of folic acid, causing many early embryonic deaths due to failure of blood formation.
The routine treatment of breeding birds with prophylactic antibiotics causes more problems than it solves.

Vitamin B12. Cyanocobalmin. This is another vital vitamin concerned with blood formation. It is synthesised by many bacteria and moulds, but not by plants, birds or animals. It is present in the flesh of all animals and was originally known as animal protein factor. Minor deficiencies reduce the hatch markedly. The usual source is now synthetic.

Choline. This is not really a vitamin as it can be made from the essential amino acid methionine. It only becomes a vitamin if the dietary intake of protein is mainly of plant origin. It is usually added to the food together with the synthetic essential amino acids.

Vitamin C. Ascorbic acid. This is a vitally important vitamin for man, a deficiency causing scurvy. Birds do not seem to need it, as experimental diets with a complete absence of Vitamin C were not harmful.

Minerals
    Like vitamins, minerals are essential to life, and only small quantities are needed.

Common salt, sodium chloride. The concentration of salt in the blood and tissues is just about the same as in sea water. It has been argued that this is a legacy of evolution. Most foods have some salt in them, but it is usually necessary to add small quantities of salt to the food. The usual concentration of a ration is normally about 0.5%
Calcium and phosphorus These two minerals are always considered together, as calcium phosphate is one of the main constituents of bones, and levels of the two in the blood are complementary.

Vitamin D is a vital part of the enzyme system that moves calcium phosphate from the bones to the blood and back again. Manganese and zinc ions are also a vital part of this enzyme system. Calcium is also essential to the biochemistry of muscle action and blood clotting.

The usual sources of calcium and phosphorus are meat, bone, and fish meal. Calcium is supplied alone in limestone flour and oyster shell grit, both of which are calcium carbonate. All the calcium needed to form the bones of the embryo is supplied in the egg shell. During the laying period, the bones of a hen undergo a drastic change. Out of this period, the long bones are hollow tubes, filled only with bone marrow, but, as part of the metabolic change during the laying period, this marrow is almost totally replaced with spicules of spongy bone, interlaced with blood vessels, which pour the calcium of the bone into the blood stream. In the total absence of calcium in the diet, the hen will supply sufficient from its skeleton for half a dozen eggs before showing any effects. Prolonged calcium deficiency produces a syndrome originally known as cage layer fatigue, initially with poor shells, and finally death.

The kidneys excrete excess calcium in the diet as calcium phosphate. If only the calcium is in excess, this urinary excretion will produce a deficiency of phosphate.

Much of the phosphate supplied in the diet is firmly bound chemically into the molecules containing it and is not available to the bird. They do not have the necessary enzymes in the digestive processes to extract it. It is usual to state the phosphorus content of a ration, both as total phosphate and available phosphate.

The levels of fat in the diet can affect the rate of absorption of calcium from the gut. Too much fat can totally prevent any calcium being absorbed. The usual breeder rations contain about 3% calcium, and about 0.6% available phosphorus.

Manganese. Deficiency of manganese affects calcium metabolism. It causes perosis; that is, slipped hock tendons, poor egg shells, and poor hatchability. Too much calcium in the diet increases the need for manganese and can cause a relative deficiency.

Other trace elements. Minute amounts of iron, iodine, copper, zinc, cobalt, and various other elements are all needed for health and hatchability, but these are usually present in the normal constituents of food, and rarely cause problems by deficiency.

Obvious deficiencies of a single substance never occur. Where nutrition is the cause of poor hatches, there is usually a marginal deficiency of many factors, often secondary to something else, such as parasites, or malabsorption due to disease. Since the minimum requirements of any of the vital vitamins and minerals are not known exactly, and as these minimums vary with the ingredients of the ration and the type of bird to which it is fed, most manufacturers of feeding stuffs tend to be generously safe with the quantities added.

Roughage and grit

There is an unescapable minimum of roughage and fibre in any ration, usually about 3%. A certain amount is necessary for the smooth functioning of the intestines, but a diet with too much roughage is bulky, and the bird may not be able to obtain sufficient energy from the large bulk of food intake.

Feeding too much fruit and greenstuff can cut down the number and quality of the eggs laid in a season.

Grit is a vital part of any diet, as birds have no teeth to grind up the food so that the digestive juices can get at it. This grinding up is done in the gizzard, a very muscular part of the digestive tract, which contracts and relaxes, churning the swallowed food into a paste. The grits inside the gizzard mix with the food, and by their grinding action rapidly reduce the particle size.

Water

65% of an egg is water. A dry water pot, even for one day, will put most birds out of lay. The water for the egg must be consumed over and above time normal requirements. One hundred non-laying hens drink five gallons of water a day.

All birds, at all times, must have access to unlimited clean water.

FORMULATING A RATION

Vast sums of money have been spent over the years in establishing the exact nutritional requirements of the domestic hen in all its stages of growth and production. The breeder ration for the hen must be the starting point for all the special rations devised for ornamental birds. Even this is not absolutely standardised, for a small hen, laying vast quantities of eggs, has a smaller appetite than a heavier bird laying fewer eggs. In order to provide the small hen with all the necessary nutrient (within the amount that she can eat), the ration must be relatively concentrated. Feeding the same concentrated ration to the heavier hen, with its larger appetite, will cause it to get fat, and so lay fewer eggs. There are rations for laying breeds and rations for broiler breeds.

The ratio of energy to protein in the diet is the critical factor for maximum productivity, and varies with the age and type of the bird. For average size breeding birds the optimum ratio seems to be about seventy-five calories for each per cent of crude protein in the ration.

Basic work on game pheasants, quail, turkeys, and ducks has shown that the protein requirements of these species are very similar to those of breeding hens, but some manufacturers add a bit extra for luck. All these species, however, do have a much higher requirement than the hen for vitamins and minerals in the diet.

As far as is known, the following specification should produce hatchable eggs from most of the species of birds kept in captivity, but if in doubt, extra vitamin/mineral mix can be put in the drinking water without detriment.

It is inadvisable to add antibiotics, etc. to a breeders ration, though this is permissible out of the breeding season.

Specification	% of diet
Crude Protein	17.53
Oil	2.89
Fibre	3.67
Lysine	0.875
Methionine and Cystine	0.632
Methionine	0.369
Calcium	3.04
Available Phosphorus	0.434
Salt	0.347
Threonine	0.642
Tryptophan	0.226
Linolenic acid	1.122

Energy: 2792 kilocalories per kilogram of food.

Vitamin and mineral additives per ton of finished feed

Vitamin A (mega i.u.)	13.0
Vitamin D3 (mega i.u.)	3.0
Vitamin E (kilo i.u.)	25.0
Vitamin K (as Hetrazeen)(gms)	2.0
Folic acid (gms)	1.0
Nicotinic acid (grns)	20.0
Pantothenic acid (gms)	8.0
Riboflavin (gms)	10.0
Vitamin B 12 (mgms)	10.0
Thiamine (gms)	2.0
Piridoxine (gms)	4.0
Choline Chloride (gms)	600.0
Biotin (gms)	0.09
Cobalt (gms)	2.15
Iodine (gms)	2.25
Copper (gms)	7.0
Iron (gms)	40.0
Manganese (gms)	80.0
Zinc (gms)	60.0
Magnesium (gms)	200.0
Selenium (gms)	0.10
Molybdenum (gms)	1.0
Endox (anti oxidant) (gms)	110.0

Chick crumbs

The nutritional requirements of the chick are extremely high, due to its rapid growth. All species need very high vitamin inclusions, but although most will grow satisfactorily on commercial chick crumbs, certain species do better with higher protein. This applies particularly to all species of quail, pheasants, and turkey. Those species of pheasant that in the wild are predominantly vegetarian, such as the Koklass, need a remarkably high level of the water soluble vitamins, notably folic acid. Turkey starter, up to 30% protein, should be fed to all pheasants and quail. Goslings and most species of ducklings can develop troubles, particularly slipped wings, visceral gout, and nephritis, if confined to a small space and given ad lib high quality protein. They must have plenty of exercise, and access to grass and other low-density food to dilute the ration. If this is not available, the ration must be diluted considerably with grain and greenstuff.

Grower's crumbs

After the first few weeks the protein requirement is considerably lower, but the energy need remains the same. It is not only more economical to feed a lower quality ration, but the birds do better.

Layers Rations

This is virtually identical to the breeders ration, except that the vitamin and mineral level is much lower, at the acceptable minimum to produce eggs. The calcium and phosphorus level is much higher than for the chick or grower. The calcium levels in layers and breeders pellets is far too high for chick or grower, and could be harmful.

Special rations for ducks, turkeys and pheasants

Many firms put out special breeders rations for these birds, and often charge very high prices. For all practical purposes, the protein and energy inclusions are the same, but the vitamin and mineral supplements are increased. Some firms arbitrarily double the amount of supplement, others triple it.

Some special rations are designed to be fed as the only food available, while others are specifically formulated to provide only part of the ration, the other part being grain. These foods are very high in protein and vitamin, approximating chick starter foods.

Most breeders rations incorporate high levels of calcium. Limestone and oyster shell grit should not be fed unless it is specifically stated on the bag. Layers rations can be converted to breeders rations by adding vitamin and mineral mixes to the water.

Renowned breeders' fads and fancies

Every breeder of birds who has achieved success claims that his special diet has been the deciding factor in persuading his birds to lay fertile eggs that hatch. Careful examination of such claims usually shows that these people are superb stockmen who, by simple observation, have noted that this bird eats grass, and that one insects, and have provided accommodation accordingly. The titbits of peanuts, sultanas, dog biscuits, ants eggs, mealworms, etc. are merely facets of this basic stockmanship, and not the *raison d'être*. They have also provided the finest food that they could afford, and made friends of their birds.

HYGIENE

It is only too easy to ruin a perfectly hatchable egg, before it is ever set, by bacterial contamination or bad storage.

All too often the damage done to the egg is not apparent until well on in incubation, and the late death is not attributed to its proper cause.

Bacterial contamination

A few pathogenic organisms, notably the salmonellae and viruses, can be carried by the hen, and are deposited within the egg before the shell is formed, but the commonest route of entry is through the shell pores after the egg is laid. The natural defence mechanisms of the egg against infection can keep at bay a very large proportion of the invaders where these are not too numerous, but offer little protection against overwhelming numbers.

Bacteria, under optimum conditions, can divide into two every twenty minutes. Overnight, one bacterium can become a million. The warm, moist air of an incubator provides optimum conditions, so one infected egg can cause the death of many other perfectly good eggs in the same incubator.

Bacteria can pass through the pores of the egg within three hours of its being laid. Entry is greatly speeded up if the shell is wet; if it is dirty as well, the numbers of bacteria entering are greatly increased.

When it is first laid, the egg is at the hen's body temperature, but it rapidly cools. This cooling causes the egg contents to decrease slightly in volume. The shell does not contract as much, so a vacuum is created in the egg, and air passes through the pores into the egg, forming the air cell formerly called "air space". Not only is air pulled into this space, but also bacteria. Eggs are most susceptible to infection when they are cooling.

Reducing bacterial contamination

Nesting sites. These must be clean and dry, with fresh nesting material provided frequently. Peat, dry sand, wood shavings, hay and straw, etc. are all suitable, and relatively free from contamination when fresh. Naturally growing vegetation, when used by the bird to make its nest, harbours very few pathogenic organisms, but after it has become wet, or been used by another bird for a second time, it can become positively lethal.

Nests fouled by droppings are particularly liable to cause infections. The common moulds growing on rotting vegetation, particularly aspergillus, can rapidly spread to the eggs.

General environment. If the area in which the birds are confined is fouled with droppings, infection can come from the birds' feet. Birds housed on deep litter, which is dry, do not get this problem, as the bacterial population of the litter is not harmful. Wet litter, however, is alive with coli and moulds. The decreased hatchability of eggs picked off the floor is such that they are not economic to set in commercial poultry houses. Ducks housed on litter give a very poor hatchability. Housing them on slatted floors or wire mesh increases the hatchability by more than 20%.

Where birds such as pheasants are housed in open runs, tending to drop their eggs anywhere, it is advisable to give the birds covered areas to lay in, and provide nesting material such as wood shavings. Hay or straw out in the open is not advisable, as it soon becomes wet and foul, and will increase the rate of infection.

Egg handling and sanitation

The eggs should be gathered as soon as possible after laying, to prevent them becoming wet and dirty. Clean eggs should not be contaminated by putting them in the same container as the dirty ones, and the dirty ones must be cleaned as soon as possible. The quickest way known to contaminate every egg is to wipe them all with the same dirty, damp cloth. Dirty, infected containers also spread infection.

Dry sandpaper is useful for cleaning off larger lumps of dirt.

Washing the eggs

Certain principles must be followed, or the washing will spoil more eggs than it saves. Bacteria enter the pores of a wet shell far more easily than a dry one.

Water that is too hot will kill the germ, but as it takes a definite time for the centre of the egg to rise to the external temperature, relatively hot water may be used for a short period, provided that the egg is rapidly cooled afterwards. The majority of detergent disinfectant mixtures work more efficiently at higher temperatures, and most manufacturers of egg sanitants give a range of time and temperatures to be used with certain concentrations of their product.

The water must be warmer than the egg, so that contraction of the egg contents does not occur, thus sucking more bacteria in through the shell pores.

One very successful commercial duck breeder has raised his hatchability 15% by washing his eggs in a very strong solution of farm detergent and dairy hypochlorite. The concentration of hypochlorite is sufficient to cause reddening of the hands if they are immersed in the solution. The temperature is 140°F (60°C), and the eggs are dipped, with agitation, for three minutes. Following this, they are hosed down with clean, cold water to cool them. It is more usual, particularly with pheasant and other relatively clean eggs, to use a lower temperature — 100-110°F (37.7-43.3°C) — and to agitate the eggs gently for three to five minutes.

The manufacturer's instructions on the concentration of detergent disinfectant must be followed explicitly. The concentration recommended is usually related to the temperature of the solution and the time of immersion. Most disinfectants are rapidly inactivated in the presence of dirt. Each batch of eggs must have a fresh solution, and really dirty eggs need a stronger solution.

The eggs should be allowed to dry naturally on wire racks before being set to hatch, or to store.

Fumigating eggs

Formaldehyde vapour is an excellent method of sterilising the eggshells. Like the washing process, to be fully effective it must be done as soon as possible after laying. It will kill all known germs while they are still on the surface of the shell, but not once they have passed through the egg pores.

Most large poultry farms routinely fumigate their hatching eggs before they leave the farm for the hatchery, as well as during incubation.

Formaldehyde is an extremely unpleasant smelling gas, intensely irritant to the eyes, nose and lungs. It can also cause skin rashes in sensitive people, and contact with the skin causes it to harden.

Formaldehyde can be obtained in two forms, as a 40% solution of the gas in water, called formalin, or as the polymerised white powder called paraformaldehyde. Both substances are safe to handle and will keep indefinitely.

The formaldehyde gas can be released from the liquid formalin either by allowing it to evaporate from cloths suspended in the incubator or pre-incubation fumigation cabinet; or by mixing the formalin with potassium permanganate crystals, which provokes an explosive release of the formaldehyde gas from the solution. Heating the paraformaldehyde to 842°F (450°C) will release the gas. This is usually done on an electric hot plate.

The concentration of formaldehyde is critical, and the fumigation is much more effective at incubation temperatures and high humidities. The concentrations recommended for commercial chicken incubation tend to be too strong for avicultural eggs, so should be used with caution. If used during incubation, there are two periods when the embryo is very sensitive to formaldehyde, and fumigation should not be done at these times, or it will kill the egg as well. For the chicken these are the periods between the twenty-fourth hour and ninety-sixth hour after setting, and from the time the chick has started breathing into the air cell until it has hatched.

For routine fumigation of eggs before storage, the usual recommendation is 1.35cc of formalin and 0.84g of potassium permanganate for each cubic foot of air space, excluding the volume occupied by the eggs, for a total of thirty minutes, at a temperature of not less than 70°F (21.l°C). If the evaporation from a cloth is used, the recommendation is 1.0cc for each cubic foot, for three hours. Paraformaldehyde is only used in very large installations, where the recommendation is 150g per thousand cubic feet of space.

Note. The use of Formaldehyde is now against Health & Safety Regulations in the UK. Advice should be sought from your Ministry before use is considered.

It is a common practice to set eggs weekly and to fumigate the entire incubator after the eggs have warmed up. This will, of course, include eggs of one and two weeks incubation age. At incubation temperature and humidity, the concentration used prior to storing eggs will be much too strong, and this could kill the eggs as well. 0.5cc of formalin and 0.2g of potassium permanganate per cubic foot of incubator space should give adequate sterilisation without damaging the eggs at this time.

As the reaction between the chemicals can be quite violent, with the formaldehyde vapour boiling off in great clouds, it is advisable to use a container with a capacity at least ten times the volume of the chemicals. This will prevent spillage. It is also advisable to use an earthenware container, as the chemicals can react with metal ones. The potassium permanganate should be placed in the container first, and then the pre-measured quantity of formaldehyde poured onto it. The incubator door should be shut immediately, and all the ventilators on the incubator opened right up. After thirty minutes, the container should be removed and taken outside, and the incubator door left open for a few minutes to clear the gas. The incubator room should also be opened up to clear the gas from the room.

Whenever possible, the empty incubator, and particularly the hatchers, should be fumigated with at least double the strength of formalin used to sterilise the eggs. Today, most large hatcheries use mist sterilisation to fumigate their setters and hatchers. A very fine mist of an approved disinfectant is pumped into the machines for a concentrated period, allowing all the parts to become covered. It can be well worth talking to manufacturers for their advice and recommendations as to which disinfectant to use.

Ultraviolet light

Ultraviolet light is germicidal, and has been used with success to sterilise the shells of goose eggs, after it was found that the concentrations of formaldehyde recommended for chicken eggs did reduce hatchability.

A thirty watt tube, placed 20cm from the egg for twenty minutes each side is very effective. This light can cause permanent damage to the operator's eyes, so the eggs must be placed in a suitable light-tight box for the procedure. As with formaldehyde, it is against Health & Safety Regulations in the UK to use Ultraviolet light.

Antibiotics

Recent experiments with antibiotics, in conjunction with washing in detergent and disinfectant, have produced a 9% increase in viable poults in the turkey industry. The eggs are first washed and disinfected by a machine, and then placed in vacuum tanks containing a chilled solution of antibiotic.

The pressure in the vacuum tank is reduced, to lower the pressure in the air cells of the egg, and then allowed to return to normal. This procedure causes the antibiotic solution to be sucked into the pores of the egg.

The major improvement has been in the quality of the chicks, besides a slight increase in hatchability. There was also a significant reduction of dust in the setters, and with this, a marked fall in the bacterial counts at all stages of incubation.

STORAGE

From the moment of laying, the egg begins to deteriorate physically, as well as being subject to bacterial attack. It is still hatchable up to a certain point of deterioration, beyond which hatchability falls off rapidly. The rate of deterioration depends on the physical conditions of storage.

Temperature

All chemical reactions proceed faster at higher temperatures. Disintegration and decay are chemical reactions and are temperature sensitive.

The germinal disc has grown as far as the blastula stage, and development stops when the egg cools after laying. It can stay in this dormant state for quite some time. At temperatures above 70°F (21.1°C) growth recommences very slowly, but this growth is weak. If prolonged, the embryo either dies, or is so weakened that it does not survive one of the major developmental changes in its later growth. In periods of prolonged cold it will also die.

The rate of evaporation of water from the egg depends, among other things, on the temperature. Badly stored eggs have large air cells; one of the criteria for assessing egg quality is the size of the air cell. If the egg loses too much water by evaporation in the store, the embryo is unable to develop properly, and will die.

The protein of the egg begins to change – denaturation - with the passage of time. This process is hastened by heat. The links and bonds between the amino acids in the protein chains, and between the chains themselves, alter and come apart. In extreme cases, hydrogen sulphide, with its characteristic smell of rotting eggs, is released, but the egg has become unhatchable long before the human nose can detect it. Any cook can tell the difference between a fresh egg and a stale one, by beating the white to make cakes, etc. This is also apparent in a boiled egg.

All species of eggs store best at about 55°F (12.7°C). Fluctuating temperatures can be very damaging.

Humidity

The humidity of the store can also affect the subsequent hatchability. If it is too low, there will be excessive evaporation of the egg contents, which will be exaggerated by increased temperatures. A too high humidity is also damaging, particularly if the dew point is reached and atmospheric water condenses on the eggs. Bacteria and moulds can pass easily through the pores of a wet shell. Under these conditions, it is possible to actually find moulds growing on the egg shell. Such an egg is doomed before the start and, if set, can only take others with it.

At the optimum temperature of 55°F (I2.7°C), the optimum humidity is between 75 and 85% relative humidity.

Air movement round the eggs

The oxygen requirement and carbon dioxide production of a fresh egg are, for all practical purposes, nil. They do not therefore need ventilation. Excessive air movement increases the rate of evaporation from the egg, with consequent deterioration of quality. Eggs stored in a draughty site lose hatchability rapidly.

Experiments with chicken eggs, in an attempt to prolong storage times, showed that the least deterioration of quality occurred if the eggs were vacuum packed in airtight containers and, surprisingly, stored small end up.

Duration of storage

The length of time that an egg remains viable obviously depends on the conditions in which it is stored. Eggs that have been rapidly reduced in temperature, from that of the hen to optimum storage temperature, will keep longer than those that cooled more slowly.

Under optimum storage conditions, hatchability begins to fall after the first few days, roughly at a cumulative 2% drop per day.

Adverse conditions can dramatically increase this percentage. Eggs should never be kept longer than one week.

Chicks from eggs that have been stored are usually smaller than

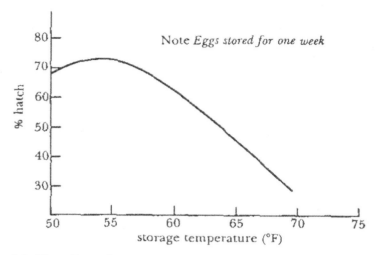

Fig.5.3. The effect of storage temperature on pheasant egg hatchability

those from eggs that have not. They also tend to hatch several hours later.

Turning during storage

The yolk is marginally less dense than the white of an egg, so it tends to float to the highest part of the egg. If it remains in contact with the shell at one point for any length of time it can stick to it, and so prevent later development. Under ideal storage conditions, this does not happen in less than seven days, but can do so much earlier in a warm store. If eggs are properly stored, and set at weekly intervals, turning does not increase hatchability.

If eggs are stored for longer than one week, or if the store is not perfect, daily turning does increase the percentage hatch significantly.

The position of the egg during storage does not affect hatchability. Eggs are traditionally stored either on their sides, or large end up. It does not seem to matter if the egg is stored small end up, indeed it has been shown that eggs stored in this position for three weeks without turning survived better than their traditionally positioned fellows.

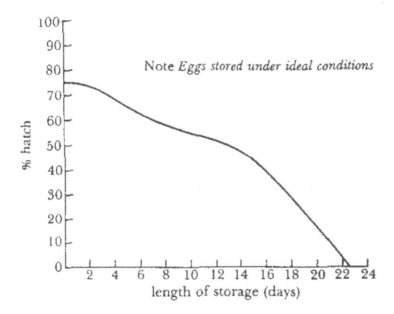

Fig. 5.4 The effect of length of storage on pheasant egg hatchability

A simple and effective way to turn a number of eggs is to store them in ordinary commercial egg trays. A block of wood or a brick is placed under one side of the trays, tilting the eggs. Moving the brick to the opposite side of the tray will tilt the eggs in the opposite direction, effectively turning them over.

Mechanical damage prior to incubation

Any rough handling of hatching eggs can damage them. Hairline cracks, not obvious at a casual inspection, but only too obvious on a candling lamp, usually cause the death of the egg. This can occur by bacteria entering through the crack, but also because of excessive evaporation from it. If the egg is particularly valuable, it is sometimes worth the effort to paint over small cracks with nail varnish to seal them, but even this is usually ineffective.

Invisible damage, where the shell remains intact, can occur with rough handling. The delicate internal structures are disrupted, and do not develop properly. Chicks without eyes, or with crooked toes and crossed beaks, are typical of the damage caused by jars and jolts before and during incubation. Eggs that have been transported and shaken about give a higher percentage hatch if allowed to settle for twenty-four hours before being set.

Pre-warming prior to incubation

The sudden change from store temperature to incubation temperature can be quite a shock to an egg, particularly if it has been stored for any length of time. Most hatcheries allow the eggs to come up to room temperature overnight by removing them from the store the evening before setting. A large mass of cold eggs can significantly lower the incubator temperature for several hours, adversely affecting the eggs already in it. Such a large mass, even if already at room temperature, can take up to ten hours to come up to incubating temperature. Small table incubators, with relatively large heaters for their size, and a small mass of eggs, can bring a cold egg up to temperature too fast. The stress of this on an already weakened germ can just tip the scales against survival.

Natural storage of eggs in the nest

Those birds that lay enormous clutches of eggs seem to have no trouble storing them. The first eggs, often over two weeks old, hatch just as well as their very fresh brothers. The same eggs, put into a store for a similar length of time, would not hatch nearly as well in an incubator. Given to a broody hen, the hatch will also be dramatically improved.

There is some evidence to show that if eggs have to be stored for any length of time, periodic warming up to 80°F (26-6°C) for a few minutes each day, combined with turning, will improve the hatchability. This is exactly what the mother bird does. She warms and turns the eggs each time she lays another one.

Not only does she warm and turn them, she also rubs on the natural oil from her feathers. This helps to clean the eggs, and also affects the permeability of the shell, preventing deterioration. The skin of all creatures secretes, as part of the natural barriers to infection, an antibiotic called lysozyme. Alexander Fleming who then went on to discover penicillin discovered lysozyme. This lysozyme is also present in the oil on the feathers, and is rubbed into the shell, giving further protection.

As the last eggs in the clutch are laid, the hen bird spends longer on the nest each day, bringing the first eggs on. The last egg usually begins incubation soon after it is laid. This ensures that the whole clutch hatches together.

The broody hen only warms the eggs on the side touching her. The side in contact with the bottom of the nest will be at ground temperature. She has to keep turning the eggs over to warm them through. It can take over twelve hours to bring the centre of the egg up to incubating temperature. It could well be that this slow warm up of stored eggs is one of the factors favouring a broody to beat an incubator.

Selection of eggs for hatching

The average size egg for the particular bird always has the best hatchability. Very small and very large eggs hatch poorly.

Poor shell quality, or mis-shapen eggs usually indicate other troubles in the hen. Often such mis-shapen eggs are hereditary, so unless the birds are of great value, such eggs should not be set.

In aviculture, all eggs are valuable, so unless it is grossly mal-formed or outsized, all eggs are set.

Domestic breeds and game birds should be selected by their eggs as well as by their conformation and performance.

Chapter 6

DEVELOPMENT OF THE CHICK

The development of a chick begins long before the egg is laid. The primordial germ cells of the ovary and testes that develop into the ovum and spermatozoa are set-aside for that purpose early in the embryonic life of the parents. These cells remain dormant in the ovary and testis until full sexual maturity is reached. Stimulation by the sexual hormones in the breeding season causes them to become active.

Maltreatment of an incubating egg, particularly overheating, at the time that the ovary and testes are forming, can render these organs defective, so that they do not produce strong, viable germ cells. This is probably a more common cause of sterility in aviculture than is realised.

MATURATION OF THE GERM CELLS

The primordial germ cells in both male and female undergo similar development, resulting in the formation of sperm and egg respectively.

Spermatogenesis, or the formation of the sperms
The germ cells divide several times to produce a number of small cells. These can grow into what are called primary spermatocytes. Each of these then divides once in a special way, meiosis, so that each daughter cell, or secondary spermatocyte, contains only half the original number of chromosomes. A further division in the normal way, mitosis, produces the spermatids. The spermatids grow into sperms.

At mating, the sperms swimming freely in the ejaculated fluid are deposited in the lowest part of the female oviduct, the uterus, and then proceed to swim in a random manner till they reach the folds in the lining of the upper part of the oviduct. Here they can live for several weeks, nourished by secretions from the oviduct.

Oogenesis, or the formation of the ova
The female primordial cells divide in a similar manner to those of

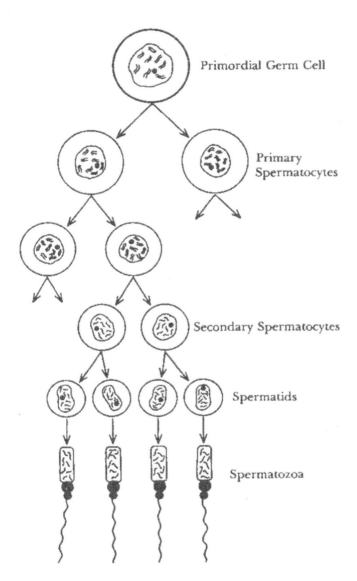

Fig. 6.1. Diagrammatic formation of sperms

the male, but only one daughter cell is destined to become the ovum, the others remaining as follicular cells within the ovary. The selected cell grows into a primary oocyte. When this divides to reduce the number of its chromosomes to half the normal number, only one large cell results, the unwanted chromosomes being discharged as a very small cell called the first polar body, which soon disintegrates and disappears. This reduction of chromosomes usually occurs after the ovum has grown to become the yolk, and been discharged from the ovary. This secondary oocyte is now ready for fertilisation.

Fertilisation

This is the union of ovum and sperm to produce a single cell, half the chromosomes of which have come from the mother and half from the father. If the number of chromosomes in the germ cells were not halved, each succeeding generation would have double the number of chromosomes of its parents.

Most ducks have thirty-six pairs of chromosomes, which permit hybridisation between them, but mandarins have an extra pair. In any hybrid situation involving a mandarin, this spare chromosome prohibits successful union of egg and sperm, so that the eggs are incapable of any development and appear infertile. Hens and pheasants have thirty-eight pairs.

The act of fertilisation occurs as the yolk enters the oviduct. The sperm pierces the vitaline membrane of the yolk near to the blastodisc, or egg nucleus, and in entering leaves its tail behind. This penetration by the sperm nucleus causes an alteration in the egg cytoplasm, which prevents any further sperms entering the egg. However, any that have entered after the successful sperm, but before this change can occur, die and disappear, playing no part in future events.

The stimulus of the entry of the sperm causes the nucleus of the ovum to divide again in the usual manner into one cell, the mature ovum, and the discarded nuclear material, called the second polar body, which also disintegrates and disappears. The nucleus of the ovum and sperm fuse to become one, and development of the new individual commences.

Fertilisation is only possible whilst the yolk is entering the oviduct. Once the deposition of the albumen has commenced, the sperms are unable to enter even if the egg has not yet been fertilised.

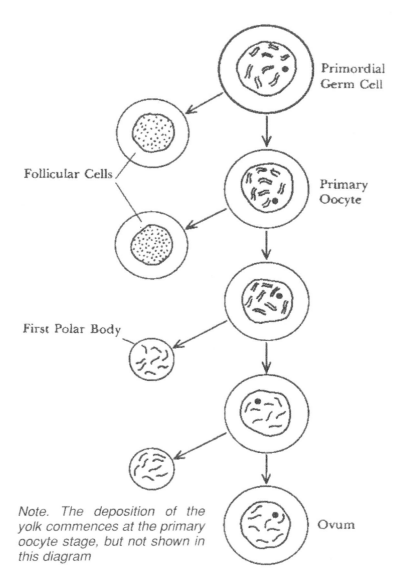

Fig. 6.2. Diagrammatic formation of an ovum

Development within the hen

The initial stages of development occur during the twenty-four hours that it takes the yolk to pass down the oviduct, acquiring the layers of albumen, membranes and shell. If an egg is ready for laying before about 4 pm, it will be laid immediately, but eggs ready after this time will be retained in the uterus and laid next morning. Obviously more development will have occurred in such eggs.

Dormant period after laying

Cooling after laying prevents further progress, and the embryo lies dormant until it is warmed up again. The dormant embryo can survive quite happily for periods of a week or so, but if the egg was retained in the uterus too long, development can have reached a stage where the normal chilling and storage are lethal. Some birds persistently lay eggs like these. They are not infertile, but very early dead germs.

The rate of growth and development of the early germ is directly dependent on the temperature. Slow growth recommences at about 72°F. Prolonged periods at temperatures higher than this in the store can so weaken the germ that it fails to complete its later development successfully.

Cleavage

After the fusion of ovum and sperm nuclei, the yolk is a single cell, the largest single cell in the vertebrate kingdom. Virtually the entire cytoplasm of the cell is filled with the fat and protein store of food. Only a small portion of cytoplasm round the nucleus is free of it. This small portion and the nucleus now cleave into two separate cells, and they in their turn into four, eight and so on, until several thousand very small cells lie in a single layer on the yolk, occupying little more space than the original nucleus and cytoplasm. Each individual cell has grown very little at this stage.

Gastrulation

This is the organisation of this single layer of cells into a three-layered structure that will produce the embryo. It would appear that the cells actually migrate into their new positions, each one being predestined to form a certain structure or part of an organ. Transplanting experiments have shown that certain master cells from certain positions will organise the cells around them to become tissue other than that originally designated, now called, "stem cells"

The egg is laid at some time during this process of gastrulation; the exact stage reached being dependent on the length of time that the egg is in the uterus waiting to be laid.

DEVELOPMENT DURING INCUBATION

In a fresh egg the embryo can be seen as a small white flat spot on the upper surface of the yolk, 3-4 mm in diameter.

After a few hours' incubation, this disc enlarges slightly, and if looked at closely, appears to have a translucent center, around which is a whitish ring. An infertile egg also has a similar white spot on the top of the yolk, consisting of follicular cells from the ovary. Close examination of this shows that the spot has no translucent center, appearing to be heaped up in the middle, fading away to an indistinct edge.

This translucent center is due to the fact that the cells there are not in contact with the yolk, as they are at the periphery, but are separated from it by a small fluid-filled space. The early development of the embryo occurs by migration of cells into this space, as shown in Figure 6.4.

The embryo now has its three layers. The outer layer, or ectoderm, gives rise to the nervous system and sense organs, the skin, and structures of the skin, such as claws, beak and feathers. The inner layer, or endoderm, forms the lining of the gut, and those organs that arise from it: liver, pancreas, and lungs. The middle layer, or mesoderm, forms the heart, blood vessels, blood, bones, muscles, kidneys, and reproductive organs.

A An *infertile egg*   B A *fertile egg*

Fig.6.3. Infertile and fertile eggs

70

The primitive streak
The migration of cells from the edge to the middle, and then down into the space, causes a longitudinal groove to form in the center of the clear area, which can be seen with a magnifying glass after about eighteen hours of incubation. This ridge is called the primitive streak. A distinct bulbous swelling at the front end of the streak forms, called the primitive knot. This appears to be the main organising area at this stage; its ultimate fate is to become the anus.

FORMATION OF THE ORGANS
Development from the stage of the primitive streak is rapid and complex, many processes going on simultaneously. These can only be seen with the aid of a microscope, and the multitude of biochemical reactions only guessed at.

The brain and central nervous system
This is the first organ seen to form. The primitive knot grows forward in line with the primitive streak to form a long thin plate of surface cells, the neural plate. Two ridges in this, one on either side of the mid-line appear and grow upwards to meet in the middle, turning the flat plate into a hollow tube. This tube will become the brain and spinal cord.

At the same time as the neural plate is ridging and forming the tubular brain, it is also growing longer at a faster rate than the cells lining the yolk, so that it overlaps, producing the head and tail folds.

The heart and blood vessels
After about forty-eight hours' incubation, the blastodisc has grown to a cap about 25mm in diameter over the upper surface of the yolk. The largest outer ring is called the area vasculosa. Under a microscope, this entire area can be seen to consist of a multitude of blood-forming islands. By the third day, these have coalesced to form a network of blood vessels, all radiating from the embryo at the center, rather like a spider's web. They all meet at a point just behind the head fold, at this stage outside the embryo, to form a single tube. This tube contracts and relaxes rhythmically, causing the blood to ebb and flow up and down the vessels.

On the fourth day in the chicken (later in birds with a longer incubation period) this tube becomes the heart. The whole process is

A *Fertile Egg*

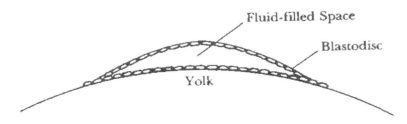

B *After 12 hours incubation*

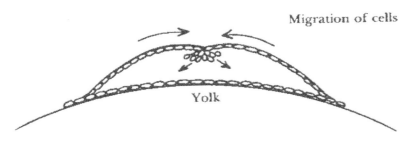

C *After 18 hours incubation*

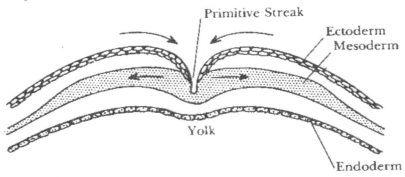

Fig. 6.4. Gastrulation

completed in the space of a few hours.

The walls of the tube thicken and grow into three distinct bulges. This creates the first primitive valves, so that the blood now circulates, and definitive arteries and veins become apparent. Further growth of these bulges, combined with the tethering of the vessels, causes the tube to fold into a Z. This can be seen clearly in Figure 6.12.

The whole heart now rotates clockwise, the bulges fuse, and the four chambers and valves of the heart appear. At this stage, as the lungs have not yet formed, the pulmonary vessels are tiny. All the blood returning to the heart is from the membranes and body of the embryo. The septum between the right and left atria is not yet formed, and all the output of blood from the right ventricle passes through the ductus arteriosus into the main aorta. Most of the circulation at this stage is to the blood vessels on the surface of the yolk. These continue to grow, until they completely surround the yolk, forming the yolk sac.

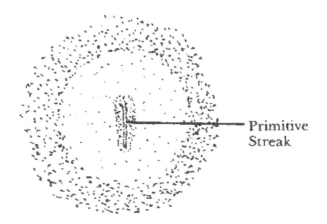

Primitive
Streak

Fig.6.5. The primitive streak

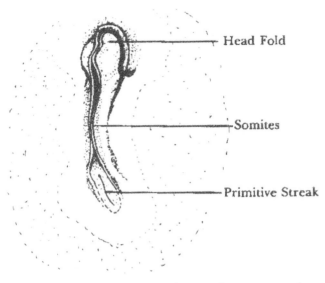

Fig.6.6. Development of the brain and central nervous system – 1

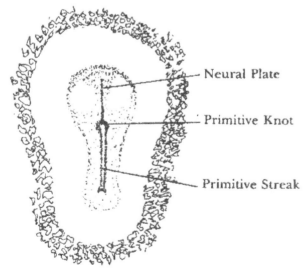

Fig.6.7. Development of the brain and central nervous system – 2

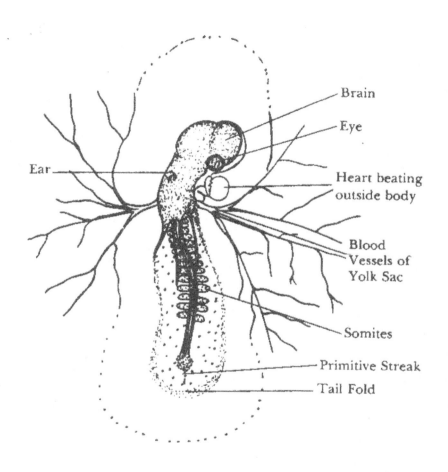

Fig.6.8. Development of the brain and central nervous system – 3

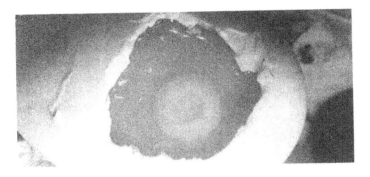

Fig.6.9. Egg after 36 hours of incubation

Fig.6.10. Egg after 48 hours of incubation

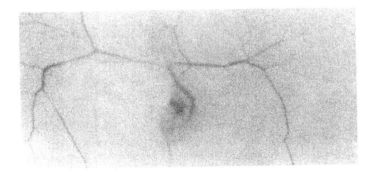

Fig.6.11. Magnified view of a 4-day duck embryo

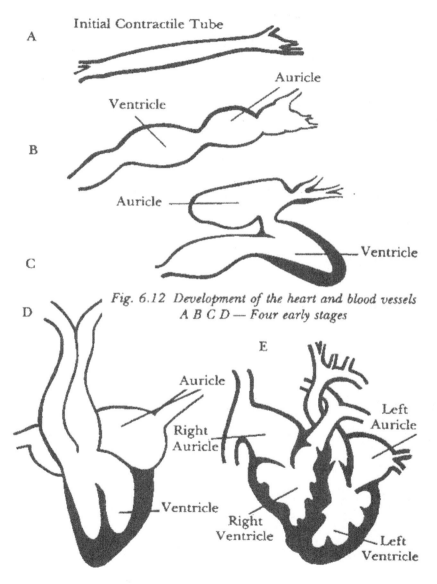

A   Initial Contractile Tube

B

Ventricle   Auricle

C

Auricle

Ventricle

Fig. 6.12 *Development of the heart and blood vessels*
A B C D — Four early stages

D

E

Auricle

Right
Auricle

Ventricle

Left
Auricle

Right
Ventricle

Left
Ventricle

E The adult heart

FORMATION OF THE EXTRA EMBRYONIC MEMBRANES
In addition to the yolk sac, there are three vitally important membranes in a developing egg. These are the amnion, the chorion, and the allantois. They are the embryo's life support systems.

Formation of the amnion and chorion
In front of the head fold, and behind the tail fold, further folds appear, that grow as a double membrane over the surface of the embryo. The inner membrane is the amnion, and the outer one the chorion. There is a space between them.

When the fold arising from the head end meets the fold growing from the tail end, they fuse, to form the amnio-sclerotic junction. The amnion now completely covers the embryo, forming the amniotic sac. Watery fluid accumulates in this sac, and muscle fibres form in its wall. Rhythmic contractions of these fibres swing the embryo about, while it moves freely in the fluid.

Formation of the allantois
A bud grows from the hindgut into the space between the amnion and chorion. This grows rapidly, together with its blood vessels, until it completely lines the inner surface of the cell fusing with the chorion.   As it grows, the albumen decreases until only a small pocket remains at the small end of the egg.

FUNCTIONS OF THE MEMBRANES
Water conservation
Prior to the formation of the amnion, the embryo is capable of only relatively simple biochemical reactions, breaking down simple sugars to lactic acid for energy. When it becomes more advanced, the more complex nutrient molecules are utilized, producing carbon dioxide and water as waste products. The water accumulates in the amniotic sac. It provides complete freedom of movement for the embryo, as well as excellent thermal insulation and shock absorption. Most of all, however, it provides an increasing reservoir of water. For the first two-thirds of the incubation period, the amnion increases in size, but in the latter third it decreases, until at hatching time it has all gone. During this latter period, the embryo can be seen to swallow the amniotic fluid. The rate at which it does this depends on the incubating environment, i.e. it can compensate for variations

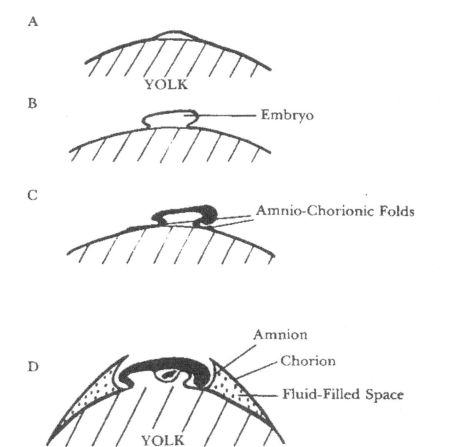

Fig.6.13. Formation of the amnion

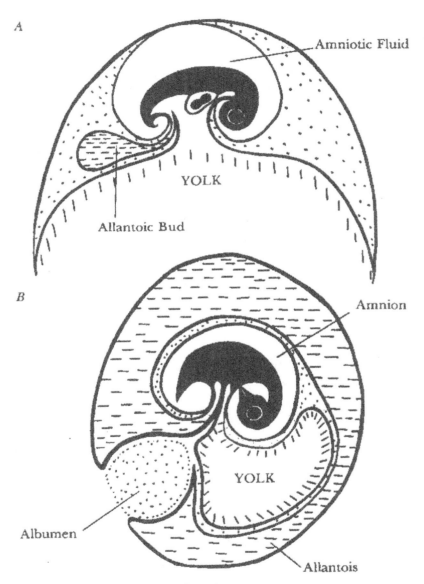

Fig.6.14. Formation of the allantois

in humidity.

Towards the latter end of incubation, the amnio-sclerotic junction breaks down, allowing the residual albumen and amniotic fluid to mix, so that the embryo drinks the last of the albumen. Incorrect incubating temperatures, or insufficient turning, can delay this breakdown.

Exchange of respiratory gases

In the course of its 21 days in the incubator, one hen's egg requires 4617cc of oxygen, and will give out 3864cc of carbon dioxide. The lungs do not function until just before hatching time, so that these enormous volumes of gases must be exchanged directly through the shell. The network of blood vessels in the allantois allow this exchange to take place, as they are in direct contact with the shell and the membrane lining the air space.

Disposal of non-gaseous waste products

Soon after their formation, the gut and kidneys start to function, albeit in a very primitive manner initially. These excretions are not voided through the vent into the amnion, but passed down into the amniotic sac. The water is reabsorbed by the blood vessels, and any nitrogenous waste converted into the insoluble uric acid, which is retained in the allantois as crystals, to remain in the discarded membranes at hatching time with the other solid waste from the gut.

THE SOMITES

All textbooks on embryology make much reference to the somite stage, as it enables them to age the embryo exactly in terms of developmental stage, rather than by the number of hours of incubation. The stage reached by the time the egg is laid is considerably variable, and depends on how long the egg was in the oviduct before being laid. Also, those eggs that have been stored for a while before being set do not develop quite as quickly in the first few hours of incubation as very fresh eggs. The incubation temperature also dramatically affects the initial rate of growth.

Soon after the head and tail folds appear, and coincidental with the formation of the brain and vascular system, the somites develop. These are blocks of cells in the mesoderm that appear on either side of the forming spinal cord. The first pair appears at the head end,

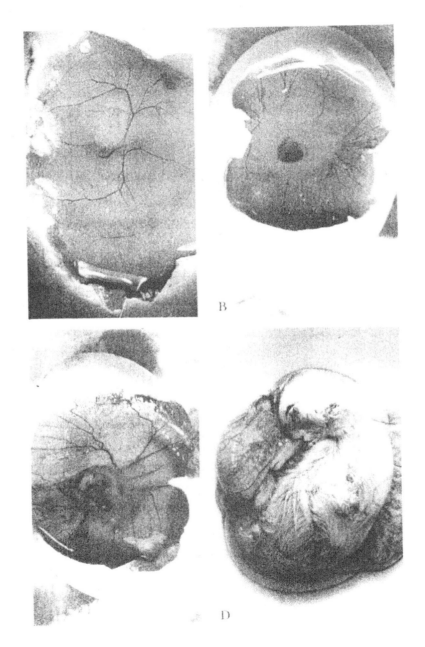

B

D

Development of the chick

Fig. 6.15. Stages of development of embryo (opposite)
    A   Duck embryo: 4th day in shell
    B   Duck embryo: 5th day in shell
    C   Duck embryo: 6th day in shell
    D   Membranes of 17th day duck embryo

and more pairs form as time progresses, from the head backwards. The first pair appears at about 22 hours incubation. About fifty pairs are present by the fifth day. They are best seen in a stained embryo under a microscope.

Embryology is said to re-trace evolution. Primitive creatures, such as worms, consist of a series of identical segments, or somites, joined together. Each somite has its own blood vessels and nerve, circular muscle, supporting arch, primitive kidney, and reproductive organ. In the more advanced adult vertebrates, this somatic arrangement can still be seen as one vertebra with its pair of ribs, and corresponding artery, vein and nerve.

The bones of the head are formed by an amalgamation of several pairs of somites, while the upper part of the beak comes from a single pair of somites, as does the lower mandible. In the neck, the only evidence of the original somites are the neck vertebrae, and the cartilaginous rings of the trachea, or wind pipe. Several pairs of somites amalgamate to form the wings and legs.

Every somite initially has its bit of primitive kidney and ovotestis, but these rapidly disappear in all but a few, where they persists to form the definitive organs and ducts leading from them.

The major part of each somite forms bones and muscles, but each somite grows a small knob on its outer part. This knob, or nephrotome, is functional primitive kidney tissue, which, from the moment of formation, excretes tiny quantities of urine. Each nephrotome grows a bud backwards to join up with the one behind, the whole forming a common duct leading to the hind gut. By the time the duct is formed, urine from the first somite is trickling down it.

A *Cross-section of embryo shown in Fig. 6.7*

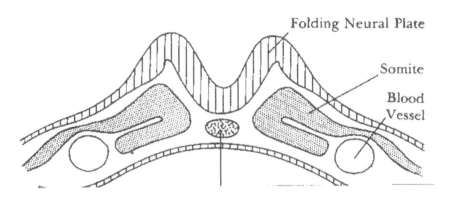

Folding Neural Plate

Somite

Blood
Vessel

B *Cross-section of embryo shown in Fig. 6.8*

Neural Plate has now become
Spinal Cord and Brain

Primitive Kidney
and Reproductive
Organs – Nephrotome

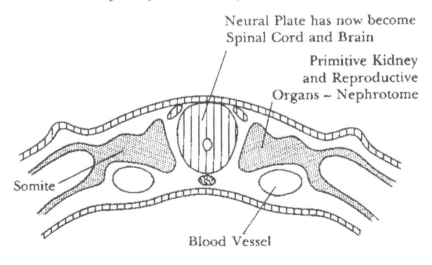

Somite

Blood Vessel

Fig. 6.16. Cross-section of embryo shown in Fig. 6.7 & 6.8

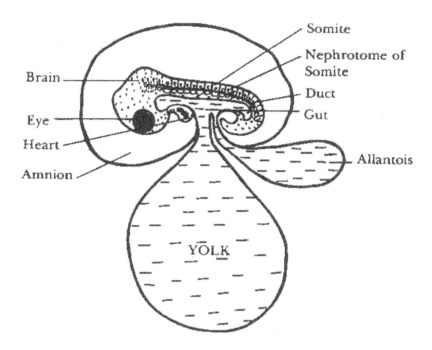

Fig 6.17. Diagrammatic position and arrangement of the somites

The urine, even from the fourth day of incubation, passes from the hindgut into the allantois, where the water is reabsorbed.

As the embryo grows, the nephrotomes at the head end wither and disappear, but the duct remains. Some of the nephrotomes in the mid-region develop into the reproductive organs, ovary or testis. The duct develops into either the spermatic cord or the oviduct. The germinal cells that will develop to form future generations are already present at this stage. Any abnormality in incubating conditions as these cells are forming can seriously affect the future potential reproductive capacity, even to the point of sterility.

The nephrotomes below those, which form the reproductive organs, form the definitive kidneys. The fore and hindgut, in direct continuity with the yolk sac, elongates. The throat and anus develop

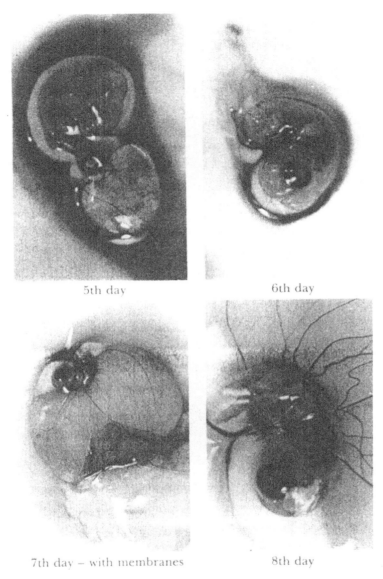

5th day   6th day

7th day – with membranes   8th day

Fig. 6.18. Stages of duck embryo growth, removed from the shell

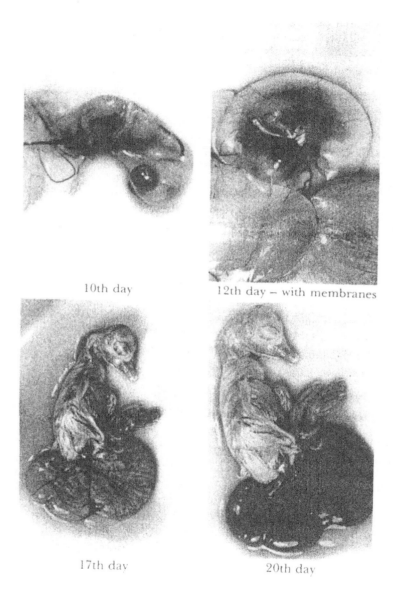

10th day   12th day – with membranes

17th day   20th day

at their respective ends.

The liver and lungs develop from buds off the fore gut.

GROWTH OF THE EMBRYO

By about the fourth day most of the organs have begun to appear. Most of what can be seen is the brain, with the enormous rudimentary eye and the heart beating outside the body.

By the sixth day, folding is complete, the heart is enclosed within the body, and the same folding has also formed the rudimentary gut. The limb buds can just be seen on the very small trunk, the head being by far the largest part of the embryo. The internal organs, including the sex organs, have begun to form.

By the tenth day, it looks like a bird. Feet, wings and beak are formed, and the body has begun to grow faster than the head. The feathers, too, are beginning to show as spots along the back.

GROWTH AND CORRECT POSITIONING

Right from the stage of the primitive streak, the embryo is positioned within the egg. For the first four days, the long axis of the embryo is at right angles to the long axis of the egg. With the air space away from the observer, the head is on the right.

By about the fourth day, while the folding is still progressing, it comes to lie on its left side, and the head and body bend, so that the tail is near to the head.

Once the amnion is formed, the embryo moves freely within it on a long umbilical cord of yolk sac and Atlantic blood vessels. Pulsations of the amnion move both it and the embryo freely all over the egg at a surprisingly fast rate. By about the eleventh or twelfth day, the amnion occupies about half the volume of the egg, and takes up a fixed position at the large end of the egg, near to the air cell. The embryo lies on its back, in a depression in the yolk sac, at right angles to the long axis of the egg, and still with its head to the right.

From now on, the head grows relatively little, while the body and neck increase rapidly in size. Once the body becomes heavier than the head, the force of gravity tends to move the tail towards the small end of the egg, even in an egg set on its side.

As the body moves and grows, the yolk sac pulsates so that it gradually slips forward and the embryo's back comes in contact with the shell. All the yolk sac is now in front of the embryo, the legs and feet lying on either side of the yolk stalk. The residual albumen is now all at the small end of the egg.

Further growth of the body, initially still at right angles to the long axis of the egg, further pushes the tail to the small end. Growth and movement of the neck tuck the head under the right wing.

The volume of amniotic fluid slowly decreases as the embryo drinks it, and when the amnio-sclerotic junction breaks down, allowing the amniotic fluid and residual albumen to mix, this is also consumed.

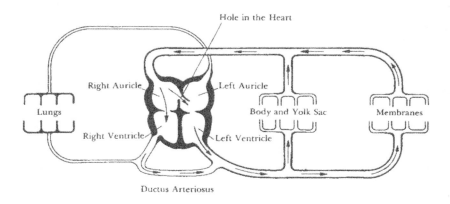

Fig. 6.19. Diagram of embryonic circulation

THE ESTABLISHMENT OF PULMONARY RESPIRATION

Up to this stage of development, the embryo has been entirely dependent on the Atlantic circulation for its exchange of respiratory gases; over four litres of oxygen in, and over three litres of carbon dioxide out. Just prior to hatching, the circulation in the lungs opens up, and the allantoic circulation closes down. The fluid in the allantoic cavity is also absorbed by the blood vessels before they close down.

The lungs have formed fairly early on, but until just prior to hatching there is very little blood flowing through them, and no exchange of gases as they are not expanded and contain no air. During embryonic life the blood is directed from the lungs by a shunt mechanism in the heart.

Like mammals, adult birds have a four-chambered heart. The left auricle receives oxygenated blood from the lungs, whence it passes through the mitral valve to the left ventricle, which pumps it through the body. Blood returning from the body enters the right auricle, passing through the tricuspid valve into the right ventricle, which pumps it through the lungs, to complete the figure-of-eight circulation.

In the embryo there is very little blood being pumped round the lungs by the right ventricle, and hence very little being returned to the left auricle. This is because the shunt mechanisms are operating.

During embryonic life there is an opening between the right and left auricle. Half the blood returning from the body to the right auricle is thus shunted through this hole to the left side of the heart, which pumps it round the body again.

The other half of the shunt is a short artery, *the ductus arteriosus,* which connects the main pulmonary artery to the main aorta. Blood pumped by the right ventricle does not go to the lungs, but passes through the *ductus* to recirculate round the body.

The blood vessels passing out from the embryo, forming the umbilicus, go to the membranes. Here the blood is re-oxygenated and loses its carbon dioxide, so that half the blood returning to the heart has been purified, and the other half has not. The small volume of blood passing through the lungs has not been oxygenated, as at this stage the lungs are collapsed and contain no air.

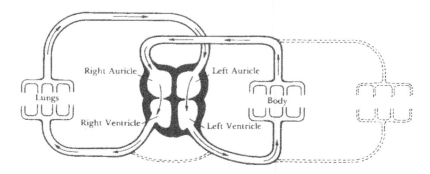

Fig.6.20. Diagram of adult circulation

Mechanisms

The first step in the change from allantoic to pulmonary respiration is a rise in the carbon dioxide content of the blood. This is because the embryo has now grown to full size within the egg, and the allantois does not have the capacity needed to cope with the increased output. The allantoic circulation is also beginning to shut down.

This rise in carbon dioxide causes the embryo's neck muscles to twitch. Because of its position with the head tucked under the right wing, the tip of the beak is pointing at the air cell. The twitching muscles cause the tip of the beak to jab upwards, piercing first the allantois, and then into the air cell. The bird is now ready to take its first breath.

The allantoic circulation continues to shut down, and the arteries in the lungs open up, expanding the lung tissue. This expansion is analogous to blowing up a bicycle inner tube. When deflated, it is soft and flaccid, but inflation opens it up to a fairly rigid structure. This inflation with blood into the arteries of the lungs expands the alveoli, or air sacs of the lungs, and air is sucked into them. Respiratory movements begin in earnest, although they have been present sporadically for some time before this.

With the opening up of the pulmonary circulation, significant quantities of oxygenated blood are now returning from the lungs to the left atrium. Previous to this, virtually all the blood returning to the heart came to the right atrium, from the body and membranes. The shunt mechanism passed the blood through the opening between the atria, as the pressure in the right atria was somewhat higher than that in the left.

This blood coming from the lungs increases the pressure in the left atrium, so that the flap opening between the atria is pushed shut, and closes completely. At the same time, the ductus arteriosus is closing, so that the entire output of the right ventricle is pumped through the lungs, where it is now re-oxygenated. The whole process takes about two days, and when the last of the blood has left the allantois, the chick is ready to hatch.

WITHDRAWAL OF THE YOLK SAC INTO THE BODY CAVITY

The same mechanism that caused the neck muscles to twitch, causes spasmodic contractions of the yolk sac and abdominal muscles. The yolk sac, complete with its blood vessels is slowly withdrawn into the abdominal cavity. The intestine has formed in such a manner that the yolk sac opens directly into it, so that the gut can digest the yolk. However, the entire yolk sac is pulled into the body cavity, and most of the yolk is absorbed, after hatching, through the blood vessels, before they too close up and disappear. Very little actually enters the gut. The yolk sac is pulled into the body cavity at the same time as the lungs are opening up, the process being completed just before hatching commences.

THE MECHANISM OF HATCHING

The air contained within the air space soon becomes exceedingly noxious as the chick continually re-breathes it, and the carbon dioxide content rises to about 10% or more. This stimulates even stronger jerks of the neck, till one strong jerk causes the first pip. The time interval between first breath and first chip in the shell is very variable, but is usually roughly proportional to the incubation time for the species, and can vary from three hours to three days. This break in the shell gives the chick access to fresh air; at which point it usually has a rest. At the time of the first chip, the yolk sac is just about completely withdrawn into the body, but not always, and the allantoic circulation is still going strong. The time between first chip and emergence from the shell is again very variable. It can be as little as half an hour, or as long as three days, depending on the species and the total incubation time. By hatching, the yolk sac has been completely withdrawn into the body, and all the blood has left the membranes.

Breaking out of the shell

As can be seen from the photographs, at hatching time the chick sits in the shell, with its tail in the small end. The neck is curved right round, so that the head is under the right wing, and the beak points up into the air space. The feet and legs are in the trussed fowl position.

Fig. 6.21. Duck embryo poised to enter the air cell, yolk sac almost absorbed, allantoic vessels and shell removed

All species of bird have an egg tooth, that is, a small pointed knob on the tip of the upper surface of the beak. This helps them to break the shell more easily. It disappears a few days after hatching. They also have extremely well developed muscles in the back of the head and neck, which also regress after hatching. Contraction of these hatching muscles extends the head on the top of the neck, forcing the egg tooth into the shell and breaking it.

There are two hatching movements. The first is the violent jerking of the head to cause a chip in the shell, which is often followed by repetitive opening and closing of the beak, as if to enlarge the hole. The second is a prolonged contraction of both the neck muscles and the muscles of the back. This contraction tends to straighten the coiled neck. Since the beak is pushed firmly against the shell, this unclosing of the neck causes the body to rotate slightly in an anti-clockwise direction. The feet also push against the shell, aiding this movement. When the neck and back muscles relax, the body tends to stay in its new position, and the head tucks up again under the right wing.

The next jab with the beak will produce a new chip just to the left of the original one. In this manner the chick moves round the egg, till it has broken off the top. A final convulsive heave allows the head to escape from the shell, and the chick kicks itself out, a wet and exhausted little creature.

Drying off

The membranes remain behind in the shell, the bloodless umbilical cord tearing easily off the umbilicus.

The modified feathers that form the down are like a dandelion seed. Whilst inside the egg, the tendrils of each feather are enclosed in a sheath. As it dries, this sheath splits and falls away, allowing the tendrils to fluff out to form the down. The discarded sheaths are the incubator fluff.

MALPOSITIONS OF THE EMBRYO

Not all of the embryos alive at final candling succeed in hatching successfully. Examination of these dead in shell will show that a significant number were not in the correct hatching position. There are various malpositions, and these have been classified according to the frequency with which they occur.

Malposition 1 The head is between the thighs. This is common, and is not, in fact, a cause of death, though commonly believed to be so. The head is not tucked up under the right wing until the embryo settles down into the hatching position. If development is delayed, or death occurs before this final position is achieved, the head will be between the thighs.

Malposition 2 Head in the small end of the egg. This is not a truly lethal position, as at least half the embryos in this position will succeed in getting out. Those that do not, suffocate. There is no air space at the small end of the egg, so that the embryo cannot breathe until it has pipped the shell. Many die before they can do this. Movement within this end of the egg is restricted, so that many more cannot complete the rotation necessary to hatching. Setting eggs small end up will give at least 50% in this malposition.

Malposition 3 Head to the left. Although theoretically the embryo can hatch just as well by rotating round the egg in a clockwise direction, with its head under the left wing instead of rotating anticlockwise with the head under the right wing, in fact very few do. It is a truly lethal malposition.

Malposition 4 Body rotated along the long axis of the egg, so that the tip of the beak is nowhere near the air cell. It is impossible to hatch from this position. Other defects are commonly present.

Malposition 5 Feet over the head. In the usual position, with the legs flexed, the feet can give a powerful thrust against the shell, aiding the neck and back muscles to rotate the embryo within the shell. In this position rotation is extremely difficult, and most fail to hatch.

Malposition 6 Head over the wing. This is a normal variant of the usual hatching position, and will not hinder the escape out of the shell. Embryos in this position probably died from some other cause.

Malposition 7 Embryo lying across the egg. This position is rare, and can only occur if the egg is more than usually spherical, or if the embryo is very small due to bad incubation. Often there are other defects. It is quite impossible to hatch from this position.

Causes of malpositioning

There are many causes of malposition. Inevitably, by the laws of chance, a certain proportion of embryos will be abnormally positioned for no apparent reason, but bad incubation techniques can increase this proportion. Some are genetically determined; but poor temperature control, insufficient turning, and careless handling will all increase the numbers. A prime cause is excessive vibration and jolting during mechanical turning.

Chapter 7

THE PHYSICAL CONDITIONS NEEDED FOR SUCCESSFUL HATCHING

No matter how an egg is hatched, be it under a broody, in a small moving-air machine, or merely one egg among thousands in a vast commercial incubator, to develop successfully, the micro environment around each egg must be exactly correct. The fundamental elements of this environment are temperature, humidity, ventilation and, of course, movement of the egg.

Under a broody, the natural instincts of the hen will control these factors, while the operator merely controls the environment of the hen. Should the eggs be cool, the hen will sit tighter, and warm them up, but if the generative heat of the eggs becomes excessive, the hen will sit less tightly and move the eggs around until they have cooled sufficiently.

A machine has no such instincts. Since the requirements of the egg change as incubation proceeds, the operator must adjust the controls accordingly. It is reasonable to assume that the incubator manufacturer has done many more experiments with his machines than the average operator, so that it is vital to follow the instructions to the letter to get best results.

TEMPERATURE

A fresh egg takes up the temperature of its surroundings, but as development proceeds, the living embryo generates its own body heat and develops the normal temperature-regulating mechanisms of the adult. By hatching time, it has an internal temperature approximating to that of the adult, which is several degrees hotter than the optimum incubating temperature. Throughout the entire incubation period, it is, of course, dependent on the heat in the machine, but in the last few days, the self generative heat may be so much that the incubator overheats, and special methods may have to be used to cool the eggs. In small table machines the heat loss is always greater than the heat production, so this is usually not a problem, but in machines that have thousands of eggs in them, it is usual to employ cooling coils. Most of the large modern commercial

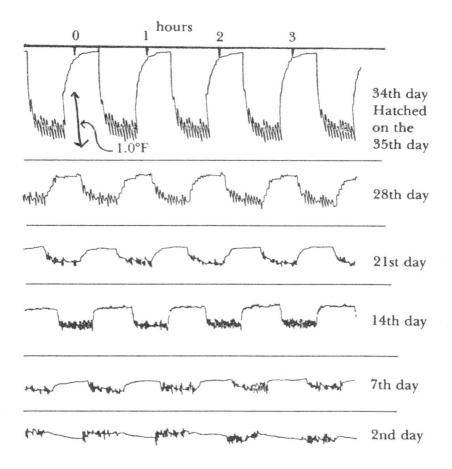

Fig. 7.1 The production of animal heat over the incubation period
These are actual recordings from a sensor bead placed at the front of a tray containing Cereopsis (Cape Barren) geese eggs. Every thirty minutes the tray is turned through 90⁰, forward and back, so that for alternate half-hour periods the sensor is in the air stream before it passes over the eggs, then after it has done so. There is no rise in air temperature after the passage over fresh eggs, but it rises 1.75⁰ over eggs near the point of hatch.

97

machines are so designed to make maximum use of this heat, using that generated by well developed eggs to warm up the fresh ones, so minimising the electricity costs. It is a well known fact that large machines hatch better than small ones, and one of the main factors is probably due to this natural heat.

The airflow also affects the optimum incubating temperature, as high flows will remove the generative heat, and cool the egg to the incubator temperature. To compensate, the air in the machine may have to be slightly hotter. In the same manner, the humidity can also influence the optimum temperature. Evaporation of water has a cooling effect, the amount of evaporation being controlled by the humidity of the air, its rate of flow and its temperature.

A similar situation may be imagined, using a group of people to illustrate the principles involved. If they are out in the open, at a comfortable temperature of, say, 60°F (155°C), all is well. If the wind starts to blow, they feel cold, and this is intensified if it starts to rain and their clothes are wet. Move the same group indoors at the same temperature and humidity, and they feel comfortable again. Now, if the doors and windows are all shut so that there is no ventilation, the room begins to get hotter and hotter until it becomes unbearable, particularly if it is also humid, all from the self generative heat of the people themselves. Now, open a window and allow some ventilation, thus allowing the escape of some heat and humidity until the heat lost balances the heat generated, and they will feel comfortable again.

There is thus a correlation between temperature, humidity, airflow, and the number of air changes per hour. When any particular machine has all these factors correct, it will hatch eggs. If the balance is not correct, it will not hatch eggs.

Different makes of incubator have different air-flows inside them, so that no two will agree on the exact operating temperature for optimum results. To complicate matters further, not all machines have an exact even heat in every part. The thermometers may be sited in a spot that is marginally above or below the temperature in the egg trays. This will also affect the recommended optimum temperature of hatching.

There are also species variations in optimum temperature that involve such factors as the adult bird's internal temperature, size of the egg and its size relative to the bird, porosity of the shell, and

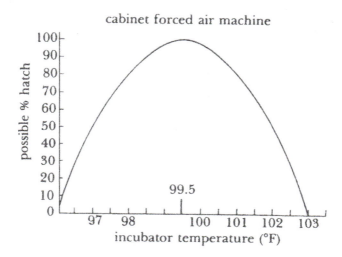

cabinet forced air machine

Fig. 7.2 *Graph of hatch against incubator temperature, airflow, and humidity being constant.*

length of incubation period. There is still a great deal of work to be done in establishing the fundamental incubating conditions needed in birds other than the domestic hen.

A great deal of fundamental research has been done on the optimum conditions needed for chicken eggs and in recent years for the more exotic species, such as parrots and birds of prey.

As can be seen from the graph, acceptable hatches of chicken eggs can be had anywhere between 98.5 - 100.5°F (36.9 – 38.0°C) provided that the humidity and air-flows are adjusted to compensate. The peak hatch of 100% possible will only occur at 99.5°F (37.5°C).

From what little work has been done on other species, it would appear that peak hatches of rheas occur at 97.0°F (36.1°C), geese 99.0°F (37.2°C), ducks 99.2°F (37.3°C) and pheasants, quail and guinea fowl at 99.75°F (37.5°C). This, of course, only applies to the particular machines in which the experiments were done, and takes no account of the differing humidity and airflow requirements.

TYPES OF INCUBATOR

Still-air incubators

Unlike a cabinet machine, where the air is moved round by a fan or paddles, and every part of the incubator is at the same temperature, still-air machines have a temperature gradient across them. The heat is supplied to the top of the machine, and as the air-cools, it passes slowly down to the bottom through the eggs. There can be as much as 18.0°F (7.7°C) difference between the temperature at the top of the machine and at the bottom, and 5 - 6°F (2 - 3°C) across the eggs.

It is obviously of paramount importance to have the thermometer correctly positioned above the eggs, and to have the correct air-flow to maintain temperature for the various stages of incubation.

The usual recommendation for chicken eggs is 103°F (39.4°C) 2 inches above the floor of the egg tray, and to juggle with felts to give 86°F (30°C) on the floor of the machine. This will give the upper surface of the egg a temperature of 102°F (38.8°C), and the center of the egg 99-100°F (37.2 - 37.7°C).

Cabinet incubators

These are of three types: the combined setter and hatcher, separate hatchers, and the small table machines with air circulation assisted by a fan. In the combined types, the excess heat at hatching is usually compensated for by putting the hatching trays in a part of the machine where the temperature is a degree or two lower than the setting trays. This has to be accompanied by alterations in the humidity, and in some machines, the setting temperature as well. In this type, it is vital to follow the manufacturer's instructions exactly.

Separate hatchers must have a higher humidity and, depending on the air-flow, it is common to run them at a slightly lower temperature.

THE EFFECTS OF INCORRECT TEMPERATURES

The detrimental effects of incorrect temperatures depend on their duration and at what period of incubation they occur. In the first few days, when the chick is being formed, great harm can be done by minor mis-settings, whereas in the later stages the same mistakes will have little or no effect except to slightly alter the rate of growth, and hence the time of hatching.

There are very narrow limits of temperature between which development will proceed. An error of more than 1°F (05°C) can produce drastic results, and fluctuations due to an insensitive thermostat can be very damaging. Since the embryo is so sensitive to wrong temperatures in the first few days, many breeders prefer to use a broody hen for this period, and then transfer to an incubator after seven to ten days. Often the wrong temperature appears to do no harm at the time, but the late mortality will be very high.

The millions of complex processes that occur in changing the single fertilised cell into the complete chick proceed to a very rigid timetable, and all must co-ordinate in both structure and function. For example, by the fourth day the chick has developed the enzymes that enable it to break down simple sugars to carbon dioxide and water. Previously it was only able to take the process as far as lactic acid, which needed no oxygen. It now needs oxygen. Simultaneously with the biochemical development, blood islands were forming and manufacturing blood. By the fourth day these have developed to form definite blood vessels, one portion of which develops rhythmic contractions causing the blood to ebb and flow. This will become the heart. On the fourth day, in the space of about four hours, this pulsatile tube elongates, folds itself into a Z, then fuses and re-moulds itself to form the definitive heart that pumps the blood in a definite circulation, as opposed to ebb and flow.

Simultaneously with this, the extra embryonic membranes are growing, so that by the fourth day exchange of oxygen and carbon dioxide can occur through the shell.

In order to survive, the chick's demand for oxygen must coincide with the mechanism for supplying it. If any one of the processes is out of synchronisation with the others, the chick will either die or be seriously weakened, so that it will not survive the next major change.

All chemical reactions speed up in a higher temperature or, conversely, slow down on cooling, but not all at the same rate. The wrong temperature can thus cause these intricate processes to get out of step, be they growth, or enzymic function. If an abnormality of, say, the heart, is caused by a wrong temperature at the critical period while the primitive tube is folding and forming, it will stay abnormal, and further fiddling with the temperature controls will not correct it. Many chicks survive at this stage, but fail to make the big change to pulmonary respiration prior to hatching.

The effects of too high a temperature: If the temperature is too high all the way through incubation, it can be very damaging, to the point of producing a nil hatch, although a proportion will continue right to the end, and then be dead in shell. The effect is proportional to the degree of error.

The embryos all start developing, but a number die after four or five days, and can be seen on candling to have the characteristic blood ring round the yolk. Errors of more than 2°F(1.1°C) will kill the lot at the blood ring stage, but if the temperature is only marginally high, the effects are not felt till the end. Once a mistake has been made, it cannot be corrected; to lower the temperature to compensate for the next few days will only make matters worse by further weakening the embryo, resulting in an even higher mortality at the end.

The chicks that do hatch tend to be small, sticky, and many have unhealed navels or even a knob of yolk sac sticking out. Some hatch far too early, but the hatch drags on, and there are many apparently perfect chicks dead in shell. As a rule, they are slow to thrive and the early mortality is high. Often there are many culls, and minor deformities, such as crossed beak, bent toes and wry neck, are in evidence.

Marginally high temperatures in the latter half of incubation are tolerated much better than in the first half. This is because the embryo has finished forming, and is now merely growing. The growth rate is speeded up, and a good hatch of normal chicks comes off a day too early. Goose breeders often notice this when they hedge their bets, and pick up half the clutch after a few days of incubation, leaving the goose to look after the other half. The incubator is set at 99 - 100°F (37.2 - 37.7°C) for chicken eggs, which is marginally too high for geese, but the partially developed goose embryos can stand it, and hatch forty-eight hours before their nest brethren, and so cannot be returned to mother goose for rearing. Had they been subjected to the incubator all the way through, they would all have been late dead in shell.

The effects of too low a temperature: Here again, the effects of too low a temperature are proportional to the degree of error. A marginally low temperature delays the hatch, but does not increase the mortality very much. Repeated opening of the incubator door to put in more cold eggs, or lowering the temperature slightly for several hours each time can produce this effect, as can continually removing the eggs to candle them. At one time it was the practice to cool the eggs daily, as does the broody when she comes off to feed, but there seems to be no advantage in this practice now.

Perhaps there was in a paraffin incubator, that had a high CO_2 level, and ventilating the eggs with fresh air was beneficial.

If the temperature is significantly low all the way through incubation, the hatch tends to be very poor, with many dead in shell. The chicks that do hatch are often smeared with egg contents, and very sticky, with large soft bodies as if the yolk sac were too big for their bellies. They tend to take a long time to get going, and have weak legs and a poor sense of balance. The hatch, too, can be dragged out over several days.

Poor quality thermostats, with marked fluctuations, will give the worst of both worlds, with a low percentage hatch of poor quality birds.

Pre-heating eggs

It would seem that if fresh eggs are suddenly subjected to incubating temperatures, this can be quite a shock to them. Better hatches can be obtained if the eggs are warmed up over a twenty-four hour period, and incubation started in a more natural manner. This particularly applies if the eggs have been stored for any length of time.

HUMIDITY

It is a paradox that there is an optimum relative humidity level in successful incubation, but that this can fluctuate between very wide limits, to a far greater degree than the egg could tolerate in temperature variation. This is because the embryo does have some control over its water metabolism.

During the last third of its time in the egg, the embryo swallows the amniotic fluid and the remains of the albumen that now mix with it. It can thus drink its way out of trouble, or not drink if it be too wet.

Excretion from the developing bowels and kidneys are both collected in the allantois. The water is reabsorbed through the blood vessels, and the rate of this absorption can to some extent be controlled.

Thus a period of being too wet can be compensated by a period of drying out, and vice versa; unlike temperature, where an even heat is essential, and mistakes cannot be corrected.

There are obvious limits to the embryo's capacity to compensate, and better hatches will result if the humidity is maintained within the optimum limits. For more information see weight loss techniques in Chapter 13.

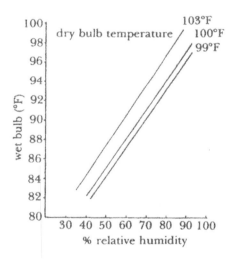

Fig. 7.3 Graph of wet and dry bulb readings at various relative humidities

Relationship between humidity and temperature

Water evaporates into the air, and is carried within it as water vapour - a gas. The amount of water vapour that can be carried in any given volume of air depends on the temperature and the pressure.

For practical purposes the atmospheric pressure variations may be disregarded, as they are not sufficiently great to affect the hatching of eggs. At high altitudes, however, the atmospheric pressure is much lower, and this can decrease the amount of water in the air sufficiently to affect hatching.

However, the lack of oxygen at these heights is a much greater problem. Fortunately there is nowhere in the British Isles that can be affected by altitude problems, but incubator hatching in the Himalayas could be a headache.

One thousand cubic feet of air at 70°F (21.1°C), and maximum saturation with water can hold 1¼ pints of water. If this same air is warmed up to incubator temperature, say 100°F (37.7°C), it will now be capable of holding nearly 2½ pints of water. If more water is available, it will be evaporated until the air is saturated again. In other words, warming air dries it.

Relative humidity is defined as the percentage saturation with water at a stated temperature. The optimum for incubation is about 50-60%, i.e. each thousand cubic feet of incubator air should carry about $1^{1}/_{3}$ pints of water while it is in the incubator. Should this air on leaving the incubator cool suddenly, it will deposit its now surplus water as condensation, which can cause problems if it happens on the electrical switches and connections.

Measuring relative humidity

The simplest and cheapest method but, regrettably, not the most reliable, is the hair hygrometer. Anyone who has ever been camping will know that the tent guy ropes and the tent canvas shrink in the rain, occasionally with disastrous effects on the campers. This principle is used in the hair hygrometer. Human hair has been found to be the best. A few twisted strands are fixed in such a manner that shrinkage in the wet moves a pointer. Even the makers admit that they are not accurate to 15% at the best, and the response time to change is too variable to be of any use, except as a sitting room toy.

The most sophisticated and modern are the electronic solid-state instruments. These, at their simplest, are thin plates of jelly-like material on the surface of a non-conductor. The jelly contains an ionizable salt whose electrical resistance varies with the amount of water absorbed by the jelly. This is dependent on the humidity of the air.

The standard method is the comparison of wet and dry bulb thermometers. To turn liquid water into gaseous water requires heat. Heat supplied to a boiling kettle does not raise the temperature of the water any higher, but merely boils the water faster, and the steam still comes off at 212°F (100°C). If the water evaporates without added heat, it will lower the temperature of the water. The faster the rate of evaporation, the more the temperature is lowered. (Refrigerators work on this principle). The rate of evaporation is controlled by the surface area and the wind speed passing over it, plus the temperature 0and degree of saturation of the wind.

A wick made up of many fine strands of cotton, or other material, bound together, has a great surface area in comparison to its bulk, and is therefore capable of evaporating and replenishing the water faster than it actually does so. The limiting factors to the rate of evaporation are thus the wind speed, its temperature and relative degree of saturation already. Since in an incubator the wind speed and temperature are constant, the only variable is the relative humidity. Changes in humidity will therefore be seen as changes in the thermometer reading if the mercury bulb of the thermometer is surrounded by a wet wick. (Known as a Wet-bulb System) Contrary to some opinion, the bulk of the wick is immaterial, provided that it is capable of delivering water round the bulb at a faster rate than it is being evaporated and that this water is at incubating temperature. In rapidly changing conditions, however, a small wick and bulb will give the new reading faster than a large bulb and bulky wick.

Problems arise if the wick partially dries out, or becomes encrusted with deposit from the evaporating water. This will affect the rate of supply, and if this is less than the rate of evaporation, it will give erroneous readings of relative humidity.

It is **essential to keep the wicks wet and to use only distilled water**, otherwise the wick will collect up mineral deposits and prevent the flow of water up the wick, which in turn will give an incorrect reading. The readings on the thermometer are of course those of temperature, and if the wick dries completely, the thermometer will give the dry bulb reading, the temperature of the cabinet. This will also happen if the air is completely saturated, so that no evaporation is occurring, and hence no lowering of temperature.

In a still air machine, the wet bulb and water reservoir must be in the same plane of the temperature gradient as the incubator thermometer, or its readings will be meaningless.

HUMIDITY AND THE AIR SPACE

Evaporation

From the moment it is laid, the egg loses water by evaporation through the shell pores. The shell is a rigid structure, and at the moment of laying, the end of the egg where the air space will develop has been determined even though no actual air space is showing. As the egg contents contract slightly on cooling, the air space starts to form

The rate of water loss is determined by the temperature, the relative humidity, and the air-flow round the egg. The quality of an egg, both for hatching and for eating, deteriorates as its contents evaporate.

Too rapid evaporation can ruin an egg, so it is essential to maintain proper storage conditions to ensure good hatchability. The rate also depends on the porosity of the egg shell.

During incubation, the rate of evaporation must be controlled. The temperature and air-flow are fixed, so the humidity of the air must be adjusted by adding water to the machine in one way or another.

Metabolic water

Metabolic water is produced, together with carbon dioxide, when food is broken down for energy and growth. Some of this water is re-used, either in further complex chemical processes in the growth of the chick, or retained as part of its vital body fluids. The amniotic fluid immediately round the chick is formed in this way. If the rate of production of metabolic water is greater than the loss by evaporation, fluid accumulates, and the air cell can be seen to get smaller as incubation progresses.

Weight loss during incubation

The size of the air cell is a good and convenient guide to the correct levels of humidity, but weighing the eggs is better, but more troublesome. An egg must lose at least 11% of its initial weight in order to hatch. 15% is usually regarded as ideal, but some authorities recommend 16%. Eggs have been known to hatch when the weight loss has been 20%.

Part of this weight loss is evaporation. The rate of loss is not even throughout incubation, but follows a sigmoid curve; that is, the rate of loss is fairly rapid to start with, settles down to a plateau, and then, towards the end, speeds up again. The remainder is metabolic loss which follows an exponential curve; that is, slowly at first, and then increasing towards the end.

It is the physical parameters that govern the weight loss, and when the two curves are coupled, they may be regarded as a linear loss, with a tolerance of 3% either side.

In order to hatch, the weight loss must follow the graph. If at any stage of incubation the eggs have not lost enough weight, conditions are too humid, and if they have lost too much, they are not humid enough.

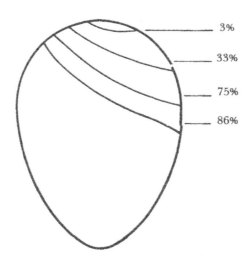

Fig. 7.4. Development of the air cell time in incubator

$$\text{Note: } \% \text{ incubation age} = \frac{\text{time in the incubator}}{\text{incubation time for species}} \times 100$$

The adverse effects of incorrect humidity

The humidity requirements of the developing egg change with the degree of development of the chick within it. There is a tremendous variation between the different species in humidity requirements, but as a general rule the first half of the setting period needs a medium/

low humidity, and the second half a medium humidity. At the end of the setting period a dry shell atmosphere helps the chick to break into the air cell, and during the emergence from the egg virtually 100% relative humidity is essential. After hatching, the chick needs to be allowed to dry and fluff out its downy feathers.

Too little moisture in the early stages gives excessive shrinkage of the egg contents. The embryo is unable to mobilise the calcium of the shell for bone growth, with consequent very small chicks. The developing kidneys have insufficient water to excrete the waste products, there is a relative concentration of the body and membrane fluids, and a residue of glue-like albumen remains in the shell. Most of the chicks die at about the time they are due to start breathing air, and those that do hatch are poor, small, sticky creatures.

Too much moisture at this stage gives a small air space, excess amounts of unused albumen, and a soft blobby chick, often hatching early with an unhealed navel, or even the yolk sac incompletely withdrawn into the body cavity. Many fail to hatch and, if opened, the excess albumen can be poured out of the egg. The yolk sac seems enormous, the membranes soggy, and in many instances the chick had actually chipped the shell before it died.

Fortunately, by weighing the eggs, or observing the size of the air space, incorrect humidity levels at this stage can be corrected successfully.

The dry shell period allows the chick to absorb the remainder of the allantoic fluid, the excess being evaporated. Failure of this excess to evaporate leaves congested membranes through which the chick has difficulty in breaking to reach the air space, and the blood vessels in them fail to close effectively, resulting in a bloody, unhealed navel.

During the actual hatching process, while the chick is escaping from the egg, the humidity must be higher to stop the membranes drying out, so preventing the chick from hatching. Still air is preferred by many for hatching, as it is less drying than moving air, especially if the necessary ventilation is not matched by sufficient input of water.

If the humidity and temperature settings have been perfect, hatching humidity is less critical, as there is no sticky albumen left, and the membranes are thin and do not adhere to the emerging chick.

However, if they have been less than perfect, but near enough to ensure that a reasonable percentage of the chicks have reached the hatching stage, inadequate humidity can stick the chick to the shell, either by its tenacious membranes, in the case of too much early humidity, or by the glue-like unabsorbed albumen in the case of too little.

The shell membrane of pheasant eggs seems to toughen in inadequately moistened moving air at hatching time. This can result in perfect chicks that have successfully broken the shell all round the egg, but do not have the strength to push off the top of the shell, and die strapped in their egg by a few strands of leathery shell membrane.

VENTILATION

The ventilation within an incubator is just as important as the temperature and the humidity. The secret of a successful incubator is in its air flow. There are two factors to ventilation: one is the number of changes of air per hour, and the other is the rate of air flow over the eggs.

Number of air changes per hour

This is controlled by the site and size of the ventilation holes in the machine. Most incubators have some means of adjusting the size of at least one of these ventilating holes to provide for the differing needs for fresh air of the eggs within.

During its twenty-one days in an incubator, a hen's egg will utilise 4617cc of oxygen, and give out 3864cc of carbon dioxide, or, in more homely terms, nearly 9 pints of oxygen and 7 pints of carbon dioxide.

In the early stages, when the egg is just a lump of food and a very small living germ. The gaseous exchange is very slight; but as the chick develops it increases in an exponential manner, so that by hatching time, one hundred hens' eggs need 4.5 cubic feet of oxygen, and give out 2.5 cubic feet of carbon dioxide every day.

This exponential production of carbon dioxide mirrors the production of animal heat, so that opening the ventilators to get rid of the excess heat will also get rid of the CO_2 and will provide fresh oxygen.

Since, in all except the very big walk-in incubators, the air is exchanged into the incubator room, it follows that this, too, must be well ventilated. A simple rule of thumb is that if the room does not feel stuffy to work in, it is adequately ventilated.

Fresh air contains about 80% nitrogen, which is inert, and about 20% oxygen. There are also traces of other inert gases and of carbon dioxide. The exact proportion of CO_2 will depend on where the sample was taken. Out in the country it will be about 0.03%, while in a town full of cars it could rise to 0.08% or even more.

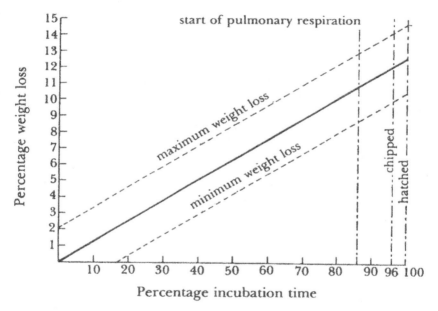

Fig. 7.5 Graph of weight loss

Lowering the concentration of oxygen in the air does not adversely affect the hatch until the level reaches 17%, below which hatches are reduced. At high altitudes above 8,000 feet, there is insufficient oxygen in the air to give a good hatch and it will be necessary to add oxygen to the incubators. Harmful effects of too much oxygen do not occur until a great quantity has been added, and will not be encountered under normal incubating conditions. A shortage of oxygen can be encountered if there is insufficient ventilation within the machine or in the incubator room.

The optimum concentration of carbon dioxide in a setter has been shown to be 0.4% for chickens. There is some evidence to show that the optimum for pheasants is a little less, and for waterfowl, especially geese, a little more. Concentrations of above 1.0% are detrimental to all, and levels over 2% are lethal. Very low levels of carbon dioxide in the first few days speed the initial growth of the embryo at this stage, but may depress the hatching percentage slightly.

The ventilation rate will depend on several factors.

Situation of incubator

The incubator room is almost as important as the incubator itself. A draughty wooden shed out in the open obviously has a much higher ventilation rate than does an old cellar with only an air-brick for fresh air. The ventilation holes will have to be open more when in the cellar than in the shed for the same machine to produce comparable hatches in both situations. This difference will also have to be taken into account in regulating the humidity and the optimum temperature. Buildings such as un-insulated sheds, greenhouses and open barns are not recommended.

Barometric pressure

As the pressure changes, so does the volume of a given weight of gas. Increasing the pressure compresses it into a smaller volume, and decreasing the pressure allows it to expand. The exact amount of oxygen in a cubic foot of air will depend on the barometric pressure. There is nowhere sufficiently below sea level to increase significantly the oxygen tension of the air to affect hatching, but at altitudes above 8,000 feet the oxygen tension is lowered below the critical point. So, too, is the vapour pressure of water. Hatching eggs above 8,000 feet is risky except, of course, in those species of birds which are acclimatised to this altitude.

External temperature

Hot air rises. The colder the incubator room, the more hot air will escape through the ventilation holes, and hence be replaced by more cold air that needs heating. In other words, the air exchange through the machine is increased by simple convection when the incubator room is cold. Provided that the heaters and humidifying mechanisms compensate, this need be no great problem. Should the room be too hot, however, this can reduce the air-flow through the machine, and can cause inadequate ventilation.

Many of the smaller machines function very poorly in extremes of temperature, particularly if the room temperature fluctuates a great deal between night and day.

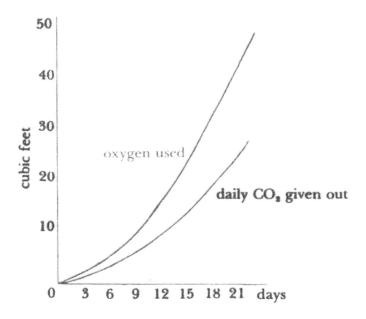

Fig.7.6.Graph of oxygen usage and carbon dioxide production of 1,000 hens eggs during incubation

Number of eggs in the machine

More eggs will need more oxygen, and give off more carbon dioxide, than a few eggs in the same machines. Most incubators hatch better when full. It is often recommended that if the machine is less than two-thirds full, the ventilators should be closed down to some degree, to build up the necessary levels of carbon dioxide, as well as to conserve heat. Before changing any air-flow, refer to the manufacturer's instructions.

Age of eggs in the machine

As can be seen from the graph, a thousand hens eggs use 0.5 cubic feet of oxygen on the first day, and give out 0.3 cubic feet of CO_2. On the last day the same eggs use 45.5 cubic feet of oxygen, and give out 23 cubic feet of CO_2.

Ventilation needs to be substantially more near hatching time than when the eggs are first set. To keep the carbon dioxide levels down to the optimum about eight changes of air in a setter are needed per hour, on the assumption that the eggs inside are at various stages of incubation. A hatcher needs at least twelve air changes per hour.

Monitoring ventilation rates

Direct estimation of the carbon dioxide concentration in the machine is the only satisfactory way in well-insulated, large machines fitted with cooling coils. This can be easily done with the correct equipment but it is expensive. A simpler way is to fill the machine with harmless smoke from a smoke bomb and measure how long it takes for the machine to clear it. A simple calculation will give the number of air changes per hour.

As a general guide, chicken eggs need 10 cubic feet of fresh air per hour, for each hundred eggs, while a hundred turkey eggs need 20 cubic feet of fresh air per hour.

The airflow through the eggs

Of all the problems to solve in designing an incubator, the air flow through the eggs is the most critical. It is the factor that decides whether a particular machine will hatch or not.

Even distribution of heat

It is essential that all parts of the incubator are at the same temperature. In the case of still-air machines, the air is not still at all, but is moving very slowly down through the machine, from the hot area at the top, and out through the bottom. All the eggs are in a single tray, and all are at the same temperature. Above the eggs it is too hot and below them too cool.

Some of the small electric table machines work on a similar principle. The egg tray is surrounded by the heater elements on all four sides of the box, at the same level as the eggs. The hot air rising from the heaters collects at the top of the machine, and as it cools, it passes down through the eggs to the bottom of the box. It passes out below the heaters, where it is heated again, and rises, causing a steady circulation. These ought to be called convection incubators, not still-air.

The convection principle can only work in a small box, with a single layer of eggs. Larger machines must have the air moved mechanically to distribute the heat evenly. Obviously, the greater the air movement within them, the easier it is to get an even distribution of heat from the heaters.

All cabinet machines are fitted with either fans or paddles to circulate the air, the design ensuring that there are no hot or cold spots within the incubator.

EXAMPLE OF STILL AIR INCUBATORS

Fig. 7.7.Sunrise Vision still air incubator

EXAMPLES OF SMALL INCUBATORS

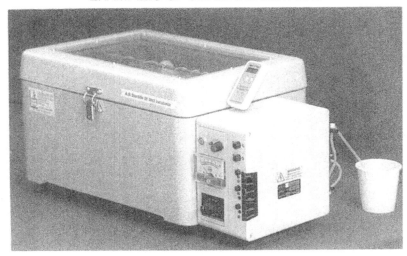

Fig. 7.8. A.B. Startlife 25 Mk3 moving air incubator

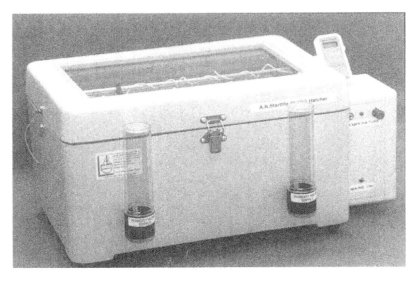

Fig. 7.10. A.B. Startlife 25 moving-air hatcher

Movement of heat from the developing eggs

At all stages, the egg is dependent on the heat supplied by the heaters. Initially, the egg takes up the temperature of the incubator, but after about the half way stage, the living embryo within begins to generate sufficient heat from its own metabolism to raise its body temperature above that of the incubator. At first this heat production is slight but, by hatching time, it is considerable, and the chick has developed the normal temperature-regulating mechanisms of the adult bird, and maintains its internal temperature at several degrees above the optimum incubating temperature.

This excess heat must be removed by the flow of air over the eggs. If the flow is insufficient the eggs will overheat, and if it is too great it will cool the eggs excessively, so that the embryo is seriously weakened, perhaps fatally, in desperate attempts to keep up its body heat against insuperable odds.

Evaporation from the eggs

The rate of evaporation of water from the eggs depends upon the rate of air-flow over the eggs, as well as the humidity of the air and its temperature. The faster the air moves, the more water it takes from the egg, and conversely, the slower it moves, the less it will take. Successful incubation depends on the egg losing about 15% of its initial weight during incubation, and a considerable proportion of this weight loss is from evaporation. The rate of evaporation must be correct. Incubators with a high air flow rate need to be humid, and those with a low flow rate need to be relatively dry.

Evaporation also takes heat out of the egg, so fast moving air needs to be slightly warmer than slower moving air, as well as wetter.

Exchange of respiratory gases

Oxygen diffuses into the shell through the pores, and carbon dioxide diffuses out. The rate of this gaseous diffusion will depend not only on the concentrations of the two gases on either side of the shell, but also on the air movement over the shell and the number of pores in it. Carbon dioxide is not only a waste product to be removed, it also plays a vital role in the acid base buffering system that ensures the pH, or acidity, of the egg contents remains correct. The carbon dioxide dissolves in the water to make carbonic acid, according to the chemical equation $H_2O + CO_2 = H_2CO_3$.

The amount of carbon dioxide in the egg will determine the acidity of the albumen. Too much or too little will alter the protein, and at extremes denature it. As previously stated, the optimum level in the incubator air is O.4%. If the air-flow is too great, it will blow off all the egg's CO_2, and if it is not enough, the rise in CO_2 in the egg can seriously weaken the embryo.

In any successful incubator there is thus a critical balance between temperature, humidity, air flow over the eggs, and the size of the ventilation holes. Should any one factor alter, the others must be adjusted to compensate. For example, opening the ventilators to allow excess heat to escape must be accompanied by an increase in the water in the machine to bring the humidity back to the correct level.

Unfortunately, not enough basic work has been done on the critical balance for eggs of species other than the domestic hen, but it would appear that, as a general rule, the larger the egg, the more heat and carbon dioxide it generates, and the more oxygen it needs. Moisture requirements tend to reflect the natural nesting sites of the bird in question. Those that nest over water need a high humidity, and those that nest in dry sites need a low one.

TURNING

The monitoring of natural nests by electronic eggs has shown that the incubating bird rearranges and turns her eggs about every thirty-five minutes. The only eggs that do not need to be turned are those of certain near-tropical species, such as the Mallee Fowl and Brush Turkey of Australia. The cock bird makes an enormous mound of vegetation, which heats up as it decays. Into this he persuades the female to lay her eggs, and she then takes no further interest in the proceedings. After the eggs have been laid and buried in the compost heap, the cock bird continually scratches sand on to the top of the heap and off again. It would appear that his feet are temperature sensitive, and he regulates the temperature of his mound by covering it up if cool, or uncovering it if too warm. Recent field observations suggest that some megapodes have tongues that are temperature sensitive, and they dip their beak into the sand on the mound and gauge the temperature in that way.

At no time does he turn the eggs, but it has often been noted that only those eggs hatch that are placed vertically, with the air cell at the top. Those that are not exactly vertical and those with the air cell at the bottom never hatch.

In all other species of birds, the eggs that are not turned regularly do not hatch. Turning twice a day is adequate for the hardy chicken which has been selected by many generations of incubator hatching, but all other species need their eggs turned at least three times per day, preferably more.

Incubation research tells us that there are eggs which have a large yolk content (Megapodes 67% yolk) do not require any turning and are similar to those of reptiles. However, eggs from the Night Heron have a relatively small yolk (only 19% of its total weight) and require considerably more turning than a pheasant egg, with 35% yolk.

Most incubators with automatic turning, turn the eggs hourly. Turning is most essential in the early stages. To give an example, a game farmer usually hatched over 80% of his pheasant eggs, but failed to notice that the automatic turning gear on his large incubator had broken down. He estimated that it had been out of action for about three days before being discovered.

He set his eggs at weekly intervals, and the first hatch after the failure of the turning gear, was down to 73%. The second hatch was only 51%, and the third was under 20%. Subsequent hatches, which had not been affected by the breakdown, were back to his usual rate of over 80%.

The eggs had not died at the time of the breakdown. They had all died just prior to hatching. Many of the embryos were incorrectly positioned in the egg, and none had pierced the air space before they died. At routine candling before being transferred to the hatcher, all the eggs had appeared live and well.

For the last three days of incubation, when the chick is moving round the egg and getting itself into the hatching position, turning is not necessary.

The effects of turning within the egg

That part of the yolk that is in contact with the germinal disc is lighter than the rest of the yolk, so at all times it tends to float to the top, rotating the yolk about its suspensory ligaments. Therefore each movement of the egg tends to bring the germinal disc into contact with fresh nutrient, which is essential before the embryo has developed blood vessels to bring the nutrient to it. Failure to turn can thus deprive the embryo of nutrient and oxygen at a very critical stage in its development.

The yolk as a whole is also lighter than the albumen and tends to float to the upper surface of the egg. It is only the suspensory ligaments that hold it in the centre of the egg, and these delay but do not stop its movement to the top surface of the egg. If not turned to a fresh position frequently, the developing embryo touches the shell membrane and sticks to it, causing abnormal growth and distortion of the embryo and its membranes. This is rapidly fatal.

Until such time as its own kidneys and lungs are fully functional, the embryo is totally dependent on the extra embryonic membranes for the exchange of respiratory gases, conservation of water, and excretion of waste products. These membranes, the amnion, chorion and allantois, are all formed in the first week. The amnion surrounds the embryo, and contains the vital fluid that bathes it, while the allantois grows to line the entire inner shell surface. If the egg is not turned frequently enough, these membranes bunch together and do not grow properly. During the early stages of incubation, their consequently limited function is adequate, and the chick continues to grow, but when growth is almost complete, and demand on the membranes at its greatest, the chick dies, poisoned by its own waste products.

Position of the embryo within the egg

Throughout all the stages of incubation, the embryo takes up a definite position for that stage. Turning of the egg is a necessary aid to these movements within the egg, and without it malpositions arise that are incompatible with successful emergence from the egg at hatching time.

Using the chicken egg for descriptive purposes, the first positioning can be seen at about eighteen hours of incubation. The embryo lies at right angles to the long axis of the egg, with its head to the right, if the air cell is pointing away from the observer.

As development progresses and the membranes form, the embryo comes to lie on its left side, resting on the top of the yolk. Once the amnion is fully formed and filled with fluid, the embryo swings about in this fluid in all positions. Pulsations of the amnion physically move it about, but by the ninth day it is essential that it is lying at the large end, near the air cell. Eggs that are not turned do not get the embryo into this correct position, which can be very detrimental to the further development.

By the tenth or eleventh day it resumes its previous fixed position, at right angles to the long axis of the egg, with its head to the right. It now lies on its back in a depression in the yolk, all the albumen being pushed to the small end of the egg. Slow contractile movements of the yolk sac, plus the turning of the egg, cause the embryo to slip out of the depression in the yolk sac and move, so that its back comes to rest against the shell, and the yolk is all in front of it. The legs are folded up on to its breast, one each side of the yolk stalk.

From now, until just prior to hatching, the chick grows and wriggles into the final hatching position. Still lying on its left side across the egg, it wriggles and thrusts with its legs, so that the tail end gradually moves into the small end of the egg. The body is now growing much faster than the head, so this process is hastened and aided by gravity, as the shape of the egg ensures that, even lying on its side, the air cell is above the point. Eggs that have been set with the air cell downwards, contain a large proportion of embryos with the head in the small end, from which position it is very difficult to hatch.

The head stays lying on the left side, and the rapid growth of the back and neck cause the neck to flex, so that the beak comes to lie under the right wing pointing into the air cell.

Once it has reached this position (in the chicken this will be about the seventeenth day) further turning is not necessary but is not harmful.

Mechanisms of turning

Where turning has to be done by hand, it is sufficient merely to roll the egg over. In single layer and still air machines, the eggs are trayed lying on their sides. If one side of the egg is marked with an X, and the opposite side with an 0, it can be see at a glance whether every egg has been turned over at each session.

It is essential not to roll the eggs the same way every time, or this will wind up one of the suspensory ligament coils, the chalazae, and unwind the other, disrupting the structure and allowing the yolk to float free, thus causing the death of the embryo.

There are several methods of mechanically rolling egg over. In older machines, the eggs rest on rollers, which are rotated by string or a chain, pulled by the operator several times per day. In another, the eggs rest in troughs, like rain water gutters, and the whole gutter is moved forward and back about a pivot. All the gutters are connected by a rod attached to a lever, movement of which, forward and back, rotates the eggs.

Most methods of mechanical turning in larger setters involve traying the eggs vertically, standing them on their points with the egg air cell uppermost. Rocking the egg forwards 45° will put one side to the top, and then, rocking the egg backwards 45° will put the opposite side uppermost, effectively turning it right over. In some single tray small machines this is done by putting the eggs into a square mesh grill or on a plastic carpet, which is automatically pushed forwards and back periodically. In most multi-tray machines, the eggs are packed firmly together vertically, point down, and the whole tray is then rotated forward and back through 90° at each move.

RECOMMENDED SETTINGS

There is an old story, reputedly true, of a hatchery in Northern Canada. This hatchery was served by a railway and, being at the end of a branch line, had only one train a week, at twelve noon on Wednesdays.

The entire enterprise was geared to hatch once per week, and the chicks were boxed and ready for the Wednesday noon train. All the late hatchers were not destroyed, but kept for breeding stock.

As the years passed, the percentage of late hatchers became greater and greater, until the time came when all the hatch was late, and they never caught the train at all. They had, most successfully, bred their stock selectively for a twenty-two day incubation period.'

In exactly the same manner, most of the large game pheasant farmers have incidentally bred their stock to suit the particular make of large incubator that they have used for years. Only those eggs that hatch in it survive to become breeding stock of the future. It is a fact that they get regular superb batches of their own birds. It does not automatically follow that other eggs in their incubators will hatch as well. They also practice rigorous selection of their hatching eggs. Any egg that deviates marginally in size, shape or shell texture from the average is not set, for they know that these eggs will be poor hatchers. Set under a broody hen, these eggs will hatch as well as their fellows.

Ornamental birds, often being only a few generations removed from the wild, have not been selectively bred to hatch in incubators, so the incubators must be adjusted to suit the birds, not the other way round.

The incubator settings for ornamental birds must, however, be based on those found most appropriate in the commercial world, and alterations made only in the light of experience.

Cabinet incubators with separate hatchers

Each manufacturer will give slightly different recommendations, based on the airflow in the machine and his own experience. The following figures are a general guide, but the manufacturer's instructions must be followed explicitly.

First to fourteenth day

	Chicken	Turkey	Guinea Fowl	Pheas- ant	Goose	Duck	Partridge
Temp (°F)	99.6	99.3	99.75	99.75	99.0	99.2	99.75
(°C)	37.5	37.4	37.64	37.64	37.2	37.3	37.64
Wet Bulb	82.0	83.5	84.0	84.0	83.5	83.5	84.0

Fourteenth day to transfer to hatcher

	Chicken	Turkey	Guinea Fowl	Pheas- ant	Goose	Duck	Partridge
Temp (°F)	99.3	99.0	99.5	99.5	98.5	99.0	99.5
(°C)	37.4	37.2	37.5	37.5	36.9	37.2	37.5
Wet Bulb	83.5	80.0	84.0	82.0	86.0	86.0	82.0

Fig. 7.10. A. B. Startlife 25 Mk 5 moving carpet incubator

The time of transfer to the hatcher will obviously depend on the incubation period, and is usually at internal pip or three days before the hatching date. The slightly lower temperature for the second half of the setting period is due to the fact that the embryo is now producing animal heat. The differing humidity requirements are in direct correlation to the shell porosity and to the natural dampness of the usual nesting site.

On transfer to the hatcher, it is usual to lower the temperature by a degree. The animal heat production is now at maximum, and the dry atmosphere encourages evaporation of the egg, producing further cooling. During this twenty-four hours the embryo breaks into the air cell, first piercing the allantois before the inner shell membrane. Now the allantois has been the repository for the bowel and kidney excretions during incubation and, in the last few days, the residue of the water in these excretions is absorbed by the allantoic blood vessels. If the allantois is a thick, fluid-filled structure, the embryo will have great difficulty in piercing it to get its beak into the

124

air cell and breathe. The allantoic blood vessels have also acted as the lungs, in the sense that carbon dioxide and oxygen are exchanged from them through the shell. About the time the embryo takes its first breath, the blood vessels in the lungs open up and the allantoic circulation closes down. This will occur whether or not the embryo has managed to pierce the membranes, so it is helpful to ensure that these membranes are as thin as possible at this time by encouraging evaporation, also enabling the chick to get at the air in the air cell.

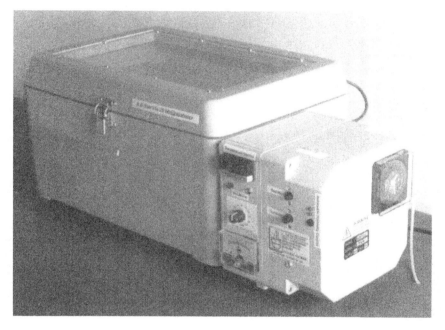

Fig.7.11. A.B.Startlife 25 Mk5 moving carpet incubator, with a microprocessor temperature control.

Once the chick has started to use its lungs to breathe into the air space, the concentration of carbon dioxide in the air space rises significantly, even up to 22%, and this is the stimulus for the chick to start breaking out of the shell. As soon as the chick chips the shell, the wet membranes are exposed to the air, and there is a natural

consequent rise in humidity in the incubator. However, this natural rise is not sufficient to prevent the membranes drying out, which could cause the chick to stick to its shell.
Further humidity must be added.

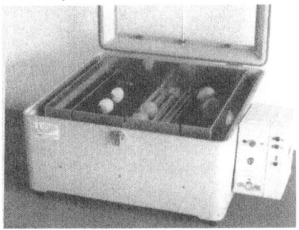

Fig.7.12. A.B. Newlife Mk4 general purpose incubator.

First twenty-four hours in the larger hatchers

	Chicken	Turkey	Guinea Fowl	Pheas- ant	Goose	Duck	Partridge
Temp (°F)	98.0	98.5	99.2	99.0	98.0	98.5	99.5
(°C)	36.6	36.9	37.3	37.2	36.6	36.9	37.5
Wet Bulb	78.0	83.5	83.5	80.0	82.0	78.0	80.0

Second and subsequent twenty-four hours in the larger hatchers

Temperature   Settings should remain unchanged from the previous drying out period.

Wet Bulb   Humidity should be raised to 65% or 32.0°C wet-bulb reading for all species.

After the hatch is complete, the ventilators should be opened to allow the chicks to dry.

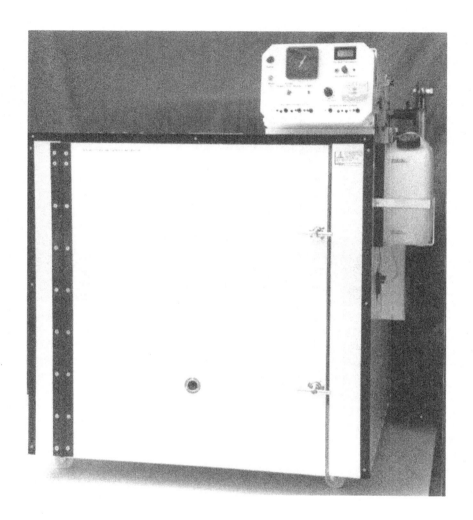

Fig.7.13. A.B. Multilife 600 fully automatic ostrich setter (24 eggs)

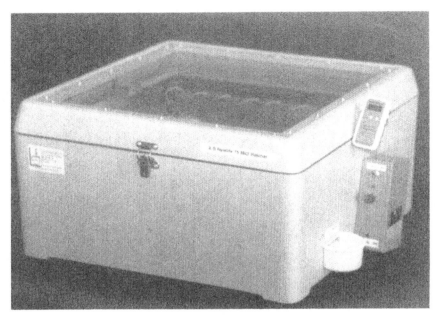

Fig.7.14. A.B. Newlife 75 moving air, single tray, hatcher

Cabinet incubators, combined setter and hatcher

In these incubators, where several settings of eggs are progressing simultaneously, all needing slightly different conditions, the settings of the controls must be a compromise.

Of course, every make of incubator is different, but the usual arrangement is to move the trays of eggs about in the machines each week, and then to move to the hatching compartment at the end, where the temperature is one degree lower than the rest of the cabinet. Fresh eggs are set in the warmest spot, usually the top tray and then, as further fresh eggs are added at weekly intervals, each tray is moved to the rack below.

Humidity in these machines is usually not automatic. They have large water pots on the floor of the machine which are filled at weekly intervals. After filling, the humidity is far too high but as the water evaporates the humidity falls, and by about the fourth day the water is all gone, and the eggs have a three day dry period to compensate.

Hatching is arranged so that the eggs get a final dry period at the correct time, and then the necessary high humidity for them to escape from the shells is given by refilling the water pots.

These machines work well, provided that they are full of eggs to give the necessary animal heat, and provided that the rituals of moving down eggs and filling water pots are religiously observed. It is very easy to over-humidify, especially for pheasants, under the erroneous belief that the water pots should be full at all times. Should the incubator be less than two-thirds full, it is usually recommended that the temperature be raised slightly to compensate for the lack of animal heat.

Today, all larger setters are fully automatic, having an electronic sensors to gauge the amount of humidity required, a mist spray then maintains the required amount of moisture at the pre-set level on the control panel.

Small table machines, with fan circulated air (moving-air)

With these small machines, the manufacturer's instructions on temperature, humidity, and ventilation must be followed to the letter. The insulation to prevent heat loss varies enormously, and the mass of eggs in them is often insufficient to generate significant animal heat to balance that lost by poor insulation.

The siting of the incubator is important too, as big swings in day and night temperature can affect the temperature of the eggs. Humidity levels are usually controlled by altering the ventilation. Working them is an art, but many of the cheaper ones are often disappointing. The usual settings are similar to the larger cabinet incubators.

Still-air machines

There are two types of still-air machine: the original paraffin burning models, and their electric successors.

As previously stated, hot air is supplied to the top of the machines and, as it cools, it moves downward, passing out through the bottom of the incubator. Felts in the bottom of the machine control the rate of air movement out, and so control the temperature at the bottom of the eggs. Removing a felt at weekly intervals increases the air flow.

The paraffin models seem to work better than the electric, for the hot air is made by combustion, i.e. it contains water and carbon dioxide. An electric element merely heats the air and, in so doing, dries it. Much more humidity is needed for these types.

Fig. 7.15. A.B. Multilife 1500 fully automatic, general purpose setter

Recommended settings of still-air machines
All manufacturers vary their instructions, which should be religiously adhered to. When the eggs start generating their own heat, the temperature will begin to rise. This rise should be controlled by removing the felts, not by adjusting the controls.

Chicken. Temperature during the first week should be 101°F (38.3C) two inches above the floor of the egg tray. At the end of this week the first felt should be removed. The temperature should rise naturally to 102° F (38.8°C) for the second week, at the end of which the second felt should be removed. It is virtually impossible to measure relative humidity accurately in the machines, so that the size of the air cell and/or weighing the eggs at seven and fourteen days is essential to gauge the need for more or less water.

For the third week, there should be no felts in the machines, and the temperature should rise to 103°F (39.4°C). When the eggs begin to chip, they should be sprayed with warm water to give the necessary extra humidity at hatching time. Under no circumstances should the door be opened now or this humidity will be lost, and the hatch reduced.

The eggs should be turned at least twice per day, preferably more, until the first egg chips. Thereafter, they should be left alone.

Pheasants. As described previously, the thermometer should be two inches above the floor of the egg tray, but should read a steady 103.5°F (39.7°C) throughout the entire incubation period. The humidity requirements are very similar to those of hens' eggs. The felts should be removed on the eighth and sixteenth days, when weighing or candling should be done. Pheasant eggs are particularly susceptible to insufficient moisture at hatching time, although it is easy to give them too much before this. As soon as about one-third of the eggs have started to chip, extra water should be added, by filling all the water pots and putting soaked bits of cloth or cotton wool round the sides of the trays. It has often been found beneficial to soak the floor of the incubator room to add that bit of extra water to the air that makes such a difference at hatching time of pheasants.

Ducks. There is more variability in the manufacturer's recommendations for ducks than for any other species. In general, it would seem that to run the machine one degree lower than the recommendation for hen's eggs is about right. Felts should be removed on the tenth and eighteenth days. The initial humidity is the same as for hens' eggs, but a high mid-period humidity is essential, followed by a drying out period for a few days before they start to chip. After this, the humidity should be raised for hatching as for pheasant eggs.

Geese. The thermometer should be level with the top of the eggs and the machine run at 101°F, rising to 102.5°F towards the end of incubation. Goose eggs prefer a more stagnant air than the other birds, so that the felts should be removed later rather than earlier — say, the tenth and twentieth days — depending on whether the incubation period is thirty or thirty-five days. Like ducks, extra humidity in the mid-period is essential, and the eggs respond to a daily spray of warm water from the fourteenth day onwards. High humidity at hatching is obligatory.

Turkeys. The thermometer should just clear the eggs in the tray, and read 100.5°F (38°C) for the first week, 101.5°F (38.6°C) for the second, 102.5°F (39.2°C) for the third, and 103°F (39.4°C) for the last week. The humidity is the same as for hens' eggs, and the eggs should be monitored weekly and the water pots adjusted accordingly. Like pheasants, turkeys need more turning than hens, and this should be done at least three times per day.

Other species. Temperature settings must be an inspired guess, in the absence of definitive information. Egg size is the deciding factor. For example, peafowl eggs are roughly the same size as turkey eggs, so will need the same settings. Small eggs, such as teal and most of the ornamental pheasants, will need the same treatment as game pheasants, while swan's eggs will need the same as goose eggs, with the thermometer adjusted to accommodate the larger size eggs, i.e. level with the top of the egg, not halfway down it.

Fig. 7.16. A range of incubation products from Brinsea

Fig. 7.17. Golden pheasant chick successfully hatched

Fig. 7.18. Cheer pheasant poult incubated and released in the Margalla Hills, Pakistan

Chapter 8

NATURAL HATCHING

HATCHING BY PARENT

The oldest known fossil birds are estimated to have lived fourteen million years ago. Presumably they laid eggs and incubated them. Today's birds have about fourteen million years of experience built into their natural behaviour patterns.

The obvious way to hatch eggs is to let the parents get on with it. This is so with wild birds in their natural habitat, but unfortunately, confining them in small enclosures under highly unnatural conditions, produces all sorts of unnatural behaviour patterns, including those involved in nesting and incubation. Some birds can be trusted implicitly to do a good job, whereas others are totally unreliable.

Selective breeding of the domesticated species has so altered them that it is no longer possible for the birds to behave naturally. Many have a clutch size so large that they never go broody. Many are too crowded even to make a nest, and so drop their eggs all over the place.

Even where a bird does make a nest and start to sit, the pressure on it may be sufficient to cause desertion of the nest, all too often after a promising start. Disturbance is the main problem, whether by other birds, predators, or even the person feeding them. The eggs only need to be chilled once to kill them.

In the wild, the nesting materials are fresh and relatively sterile. In captivity, all too often the site is soiled with droppings, and the nesting material rotting and riddled with aspergillus and other nasties.

In most cases, even if the bird does successfully hatch off her brood, she loses most of them from cold and hunger, as they trail after her while she desperately tries to find the space and peace to brood and feed them. Geese and swans tend to be successful parents, ducks tend to hatch successfully, and then lose most of them, whilst pheasants are usually hopeless at nesting, hatching and rearing. There are, of course, exceptions to every rule.

Unless the bird can be guaranteed peace and quiet, it is always better to pick up the eggs and hatch them by other means.

Broodiness

As the bird's metabolism undergoes a profound change when it starts to lay eggs, so further profound changes occur as it goes broody after the clutch is completed. This change is induced by the secretion of prolactin by the pituitary gland. The basal metabolic rate drops, and its internal temperature falls by a degree or two. The entire behaviour pattern alters as the bird becomes immobile on the nest, and a most uncharacteristic aggression develops to any disturber or predator. The breast feathers loosen and come out, often being plucked to form the down that lines the nest. The skin so exposed, the brood patch, enables the bird to warm the eggs more effectively. As incubation proceeds, this broodiness becomes more apparent.

Some males share in the incubation duties, and these males are influenced by prolactin secretion.

Monitoring natural nests

Several studies have been made over the years of the behaviour of sitting wild birds, and sensors placed in the nests to record the micro-environment in it. The results are, at first, confusing, but have led to a great deal of knowledge and a better understanding of what actually happens inside the nest.

The temperature recorded by the sensors varies according to where they are in the nest. As a general rule, the eggs in the centre of the nest are warmer than those around the outside. That part of the egg touching the bird is at the same temperature as the skin of the bird, whilst that part touching the floor of the nest is considerably cooler up to 18°F (10°C) lower. As incubation proceeds, the floor of the nest gradually becomes warmer. Studies with these electronic eggs have shown that the bird turns the eggs about every twenty to thirty-five minutes, rolling the cooler eggs from the periphery into the middle, and the cooler, lower surface of the eggs to the top.

The picture is confused by the fact that as incubation proceeds, the eggs themselves generate heat. Just before hatching time, their temperature is several degrees above the optimum incubation temperature. A sensor touching an egg will give a higher reading than one not touching.

The reading obtained from the centre of an electronic egg can be erroneous, as it will depend on the thermal conductivity of the filling of the egg. For example, if one end of a copper rod is heated, whilst the other end is held in the hand, it soon becomes too hot to handle. A piece of wood of the same dimensions can be held for a long time whilst the other end burns merrily.

The bird controls the temperature of the nest entirely instinctively. Those eggs which feel cool are rolled into the centre, and the warmer ones pushed to the outside. If the whole nest is cool, she sits tighter, and if it becomes too warm, - heat is allowed to escape.

As a generalisation, small eggs are maintained at about 99.5°F (37.5°C) at the centre of the egg, and larger ones about $^1/_2$ -1°F (0.25 - 0.5°C) lower.

The humidity recorded during incubation showed enormous variations, depending on the site of the nest, the prevailing weather conditions, and whether the bird frequented water or not. The average figure is about 60% relative humidity.

Most birds moved their eggs every twenty to thirty-five minutes. The eggs were not turned completely, but moved in a random manner around the nest, so that some could not be said to be turned at all, merely stirred.

The absences from the nest varied with the state of incubation, and the weather. In the early stages, absences were of very short duration, but towards the end, and particularly in hot weather, they became very much longer. Where nests were lined with considerable quantities of down, the temperature of the eggs fell very little during the bird's absences to feed. The nest was usually left at the same time each day, most commonly in the late afternoon.

HATCHING BY BROODY HEN

Until the advent of large-scale intensive poultry units, all hatching was done by broody hens. The sheer volume of hatching eggs for those units meant that incubation had to be come mechanical. Specific breeding of hybrid strains for either meat or egg production made the tendency to broodiness an undesirable characteristic to be eliminated from the strain. Broody hens are now virtually unobtainable from the commercial world.

Broody hens are still used by a few aviculturists, and those who rear a few game birds for shooting, mainly because the incubator manufacturers, who used to make excellent machines holding a hundred or so chicken eggs, have followed the poultry industry by producing large game setters. Incubators and brooders holding only a few eggs were not commercial, so became the cinderellas of the industry. They tended to be made to a price and not to a specification; only in recent years has research improved their designs. Because of this basic unreliability, many aviculturists and gamekeepers found them disappointing and stuck to their broody hens. Things have now changed for the better.

There is no doubt that a properly managed broody hen is still the finest incubator yet developed. It also has the advantage that it is a superb brooder as well after the chicks have hatched. The main disadvantages are the cost of maintaining a flock of hens to ensure sufficient broodies at the right time, the ever present danger of the hen transmitting disease, and the work involved in looking after them.

Types of broody hen

Broody hens come in all shapes and sizes. The weight can vary from a $^3/_4$lb bantam, to a 7-8 lb hen. The feather structure of the hen can be the hard closeness of the Game, the soft looseness of the Silkie or anything in between. The shape too can vary. Game type hens carry their meat on their breasts, like a dimple breasted turkey, with little flesh on their legs. These are usually referred to as hot hens, as they have much more meat to put over the eggs. Wedge shaped hens, with a keel bone like a V, carry the meat on their legs, and tend to incubate cooler. These cooler hens tend to have loose feathers, and fluffy legs.

As a general rule, the bigger the egg, the hotter the hen needed. All diving ducks need a hot hen. Big eggs under light cool hens don't hatch well. Goose eggs do not need a hot hen, but they do need a large one.

Small eggs, such as the Teal, Wigeon, Pintail, and most of the pheasant and partridge family need an average type hen. They do not hatch well under a large hot hen.

The traditional gamekeeper's bird is a Game crossed with a Silkie. They tend to be uniform and foolproof. The Game is an excellent mother, but wild by nature, and is generally hot. It improves as a broody with age, being at its best when over three years old. The Silkie is exceptionally tame, incubates cooler, goes broody at only five months old, and behaves impeccably. The cross is a sensible bird, with average temperature, and goes broody early in life, and can be relied on for many years, often rearing two or three clutches each year. It is the ideal bird for the beginner or amateur.

Many other breeds of bantam and hen make excellent broodies. Every successful breeder who keeps his own special flock of hens for broodies, only breeds replacements from those hens which have served him well. The hens are all shapes, sizes and colours, but most have some Silkie and Game in their makeup.

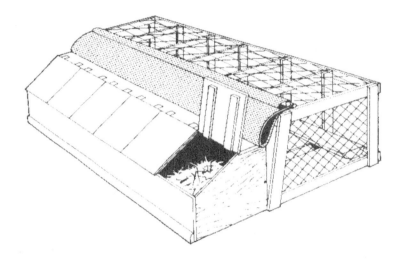

Fig.8.1. Diagram of broody nest boxes

The sitting box

A broody hen must have peace and quiet. Darkness or subdued lighting improves the steadiness of the hen. Any old box of the right size will do, for unlike their human counterparts, broodies are not house proud. If the box is too small, the hen will be cramped and uncomfortable. She will probably break some of the eggs trying to turn round, and if in real discomfort will give up trying to sit. If the box is too large, eggs can roll away from her and get chilled, or the hen may make another nest, leaving most of the eggs in the original. The standard size is 14 inches square, by 14 inches high.

The entrance to the box can either be from the front, or from the top. The disadvantage of the top opening box is that a clumsy large hen can break eggs when jumping in. However, many breeders prefer boxes of this type, as they place the hen back in. The easiest way to make a sitting box is to put a sack over the front of an old orange box, held in place by two bricks. This has two compartments of just the right size when laid on its side.

A coop and run will do just as well, the hen being confined to the run when off for its daily exercise. This does have the problem of droppings rapidly fouling up the run, increasing the likelihood of infecting the eggs. A solution is to raise the whole structure on legs, and provide a wire netting floor to the run; the droppings can then be cleaned up without disturbing the hen.

The box must, of course, have some ventilation. If many hens are sitting simultaneously, rows of boxes can be made as one structure.

Siting the sitting boxes

There are many sound arguments why the sitting boxes should be sited in a shed, or out in the open, or on the ground, or off the floor. The site of the box will determine the humidity within the nest.

Boxes in the open The box will be exposed to the weather, and full sun shining on it can make it very hot and uncomfortable for the hen. Also the constant drip of rain on her back is not the best encouragement. However, the natural moisture of the ground is the best way of supplying the necessary humidity to the nest. Outdoor boxes should be set in the shade, such as under a tree, and be totally waterproof from the top. Burrowing moles and rats can wreak havoc, so it is advisable to have wire netting buried under the nest to prevent this. If the hens have complete freedom when removed from the box for their daily feed and exercise, an unsteady or slightly wild hen can be a nuisance to get back on the box before the eggs get chilled. Under these circumstances, it is prudent to tether the birds by a string to one leg, anchored to a suitable peg, so that they can't get too far away. This will also prevent fighting when several birds are let out together. They soon get used to it and do not struggle after the first day or two, if they are well and truly broody. Birds that are only just going broody, or are wild and temperamental by nature, can be put off by this and will not sit properly.

Boxes in a shed. Housing the boxes in a shed does give total independence from the weather; the birds can be let off quite happily when it is raining. Neither can they escape. It is much easier to drive a reluctant bird back on its nest in the confines of a shed. There is no natural moisture in a shed, so whether the boxes are sited on the floor for convenience, or raised off the ground for hygiene, extra humidity must be added to the nest. It is an art knowing when to add water, and how much. Wrong quantities, or wrong timing, can ruin the hatch. Constant monitoring of the air cells is important. The eggs of those birds, such as the Goldeneye, which naturally nest off the ground, need a hen off the ground and little moisture. Eggs laid on damp, marshy ground need more humidity.

Making the nest

The traditional nest is constructed by placing an upturned turf on the floor of the box, and then making a nest of hay on top of that. The shape of the nest is determined by the shape and size of the hen that sits on it. In practice, it matters little what the nest material is, provided that it is clean and fresh. Mixtures of dry sand, peat, fresh hay or straw are all acceptable, and there must be at least 3 inches of material at the bottom of the nest. No matter how well the nest appears to be constructed, the hen will rearrange it to her satisfaction. If the corners of the box are not packed firmly, and if there is less than 3 inches of material in the base to play with, the hen can put the entire contents of the nest box out to the sides and scrape her way down to the hard floor. Eggs are easily cracked and broken in such a situation.

Management of the broody

It is very easy to tell whether a hen is broody or not; the behaviour of the bird is quite characteristic. It is not always so easy when a hen is desperately needed, and the bird has only just started to sit. Any hen in the laying pen sitting in the nesting boxes by day is probably just laying an egg. If it is still sitting after dark, it is probably going broody. If a hand is inserted under the sitting bird, with the palm uppermost and the fingers opened and gently pushed into the bird, the broody bird will ruffle her feathers and emit the characteristic noise. A non-broody bird will not react. Any hen that flies off squawking is not to be trusted yet.

Broody hens should never be moved from the laying pen to the sitting boxes in daylight. This will upset most of them, particularly if they have only been broody for a short while. The move must always be done in the dark, and the birds handled with great care.

For the first few days, until she is thoroughly settled, it is advisable to give the hen dummy eggs to sit on.

All hens, when moved to the sitting boxes, should be given a routine health inspection. Any without a bright beady eye, or who are excessively thin or showing signs of disease such as diarrhoea, or breathing troubles, should not be used. Any feathers on the legs should be cut off close to the leg, as these can cause accidents when taking her off the nest.

Scaly legs must be treated with a suitable mite spray, as this can cause discomfort and is invariably passed on to the chicks. This treatment should really have been given before the bird went broody.

The nest box and the broody should be liberally treated with a suitable insecticide powder. Particular attention should be given to the vent area and under the wings, as well as ruffling the feathers against the direction of feather growth, and getting the powder right on to the skin. A hen tormented by insect bites is restless.

Daily management

The hens should be let off the sitting boxes once each day, and always at the same time. They are creatures of habit and behave better if they have a strict routine. During the time off the nest, each bird should be seen to feed, drink and empty its bowels. Most birds know instinctively when they have been off long enough. On a cold day, when the eggs are newly set, three or four minutes is long enough, or the eggs will get fatally chilled. Eggs near to hatching, on a warm day, will come to no harm for up to half an hour.

In a shed full of broodies, any newcomers will tend to be bullied, which can prevent them from performing their natural functions, and makes them wild and unwilling to co-operate. It is advisable to let these out first, so that they are ready to go back on the nest by the time that the oldtimers are ready to demonstrate their natural superiority.

Handling broodies is an art. To some it comes naturally, to some it can be taught, and to some it never comes at all. The ladies of the household are usually better at it than the men. The ladies know which lot of hens to let off together, and which not to. Men tend to be time and motion experts, and, when the hens are let out in mathematical blocks and chaos results, go off and design individual coops and runs off the ground, or tethering sites, where they can't fight and escape.

Shutting the door of each broody box whilst the hens are off ensures that each hen has sufficient time, and can't go back on to the wrong nest. When their time is up, most hens are waiting to go back on or can be gently driven into the box. Patience and gentleness are essential in the round up. A shed full of squawking flying hens, being chased by an irate man with a landing net, does not produce the best results.

The hens must be lifted off the nest very gently, after ensuring that no eggs are tucked up under the wings. Any bird that has fouled the nest is either sick, going off broody, or did not have enough time off the day before. Any bird that does not look well should be discarded and its eggs given to another.

All the hens should have time and peace to fill their crops with food. Pellets or meal tend to produce watery droppings, so it is better to feed whole mixed grain with some maize. This gives a dry, solid dropping, and is high in energy.

They must also have clean fresh water. If a tray of dry soil is available, the birds really enjoy a dust bath. A little pyrethrum powder in this will help to keep them free of parasites. Some grit should always be provided when the diet is wholly grain.

Scrupulous hygiene should be observed and all droppings cleaned up. If the sitting boxes are all off the ground, hosing down the floor will not only lessen the bacterial build-up in the shed, but will also increase the humidity. The eggs should be candled once a week and, if necessary, the nests damped down. Most ducks benefit from a spray of warm water towards hatching time, and all eggs set under hens off the ground should be moistened about the time of the first chip.

Once the eggs begin to hatch, the bird should be left completely alone until the hatch is complete. The spectre of the broody that sits impeccably and then kills every chick as it hatches, haunts most broody sheds. Unless the bird is a tried and trusted old matron, it is far safer to remove most of the eggs to an incubator for hatching, returning the chicks to the bird under supervision. If possible, she should be allowed to hatch one or two non-valuable eggs as an indicator.

Humidity control depends very much on the site of the box and the weather. Birds sitting directly on the ground usually need no water added to the area, except in a very dry, hot season. Nests containing waterfowl eggs usually need more moisture if the box is indoors, particularly if it is also off the ground.

Large eggs are not usually turned sufficiently by the hen, so it is always a good thing to turn them over each time the broody is taken off.

Eggs of mixed parentage, and multi-incubation ages, never hatch well if set together under one hen. It is always preferable to put under a hen eggs that are all due to hatch together.

Combined broody and incubator hatching

There is no doubt that the broody hen will beat most incubators, and it is in the first few days that she does it. There are never enough broody hens at the critical times.

Many breeders put their eggs under a broody for the first week, then transfer the good ones to an incubator, and give the hen a fresh lot of eggs. After these have been incubated for a week, they too go to the incubator, and the hen is given a third lot. When the first batch chip, they are returned to the hen to hatch. The large number of infertile eggs in aviculture usually ensures that there are enough hens for hatching.

Infra-red lamps have transformed the rearing methods, so that fewer breeders each year are using hens to rear. The hens incubate fresh eggs week after week. It is not advisable to keep a hen sitting longer than four weeks as it takes too much out of them, and most, after this time, give up anyway.

Selecting a hen for the different species

In theory, there is a type of broody hen that is ideal for each different species of eggs. In practice, the choice is all too often limited to whichever hen is available.

Best results are obtained by matching the size of the hen to the size of the eggs, but even the very large hens will still hatch small pheasant eggs quite satisfactorily. These large hens can cover up to twenty-four pheasant-size eggs, but a bantam can only manage about a dozen. A large hen can manage four or five goose eggs, but they will need extra turning.

Diving ducks must have a large hot hen. A 5 lb game hen is all breast in the hand, but a bantam is all keel bone and feather. These diving ducks; Stifftails, Goldeneye, Scoters, Scaup, and Tufted, are much more developed at hatching. They do not get any brooding on open water. The eggs have a very large yolk in proportion to the white, and the egg is enormous in proportion to the bird. These eggs don't hatch under a cool hen; most die in the last week of incubation. Under a hot hen, they hatch well, but do need more water added to the nest for the second half of incubation.

The choice of broody for the eggs is also influenced by the maternal instincts of the hen for rearing. Game hens use their feet actively to find food for active chicks. These birds will kick immobile Emperor goslings all over the place. Silkies and Houdans are very quiet, and much more suitable for this.

Teal, Mandarins, Carolinas and all the smaller pheasants need a lot of brooding.

The best all round pure breed is the Sumatran game. It is the best parent, with a highly developed maternal instinct. It is a reasonably hot hen, and quite easy to handle. Their big disadvantage is the fact that they won't accept anything that they haven't hatched.

Some birds are reputed to sit tighter than others. The tightness of sitting depends, in fact, on the atmospheric temperature. The eggs under tight sitters need more turning.

When a little scientific measurement is applied to the myths and folklore that form so much of the art of hatching by broody hen, certain things become apparent. The broody hen is reputed to have a higher temperature than the non-broody. The thermometer says that the broody's temperature is 2°F lower. It feels hotter, because the feathers have been shed from the breast. The temperature of a hot hen is identical to that of a cool one; it merely has a larger expanse of bare breast to put on the eggs, so transferring more heat to the eggs, than the bare keel bone and feathered legs of the cool one.

Chapter 9

INCUBATOR HATCHING

HISTORICAL ASPECTS

There is nothing new under the sun. The modern poultry industry, with its production of millions of birds from centralized massive incubators, is not a new technology. The men who built the pyramids also built incubators. Even before the time of Moses, hatcheries with a capacity of ninety thousand were in full production. A few of these hatcheries are still operative, and even as late as the 1950s, were producing almost 90% of all the chicks in Egypt.

The design and construction of these hatcheries was ingenious but simple. The eggs lay on the floor of a cylindrical, brick building. Two to three feet above the eggs was a trough-like platform encircling the inner wall, within which burned a perpetual fire of camel dung. Air was drawn in through an opening at ground level, passed through the central hole in the ring of fire, and out through a hole in the dome-shaped roof.

Double rows of these incubating ovens faced on to a central corridor. Openings in the roof and ends of this corridor admitted light and ventilation.

The temperature of the eggs was measured by placing them against the eye-lids, and controlled by stoking or raking the fires. Humidity requirements and air cell size were judged by the sound made by rolling two eggs together in one hand.

Ancient records tell us that they custom hatched, returning two chicks for every three eggs brought in. their profit was all the hatch above 70%.

The Egyptians did not, however, have a monopoly on egg hatching. Their Chinese counterparts had developed two very successful methods by at least 1,000 B.C.

The first, and simplest, used the heat of rotting manure. The eggs were placed in a mixture of chopped straw and rice hulls on top of the manure; it appears to have been moderately successful.

The second method, more widely used and still functional today, was just as ingenious as the Egyptian hatchery. The basic structure was again a cylindrical building, but the fire was on the floor, with the eggs contained in an inverted cone above it, partially filled with ashes. Placed on the ashes were egg baskets made of woven straw. The eggs were contained in muslin bags, the whole being covered in an insulating layer of rice hulls. A straw thatch roof, shaped like the traditional coolie's hat, completed the insulation, and kept out the rain.

Every seven days a fresh bag of eggs was added to each basket, and the bags were continually moved about to turn the eggs. After the first three weeks of the hatching season, the fire was allowed to go out; the self-generative heat of the eggs kept the process going.

They had also developed the art of candling, for clear eggs were removed on the third day and sold for normal consumption.

The Greeks were not to be outdone, for Aristotle described in detail a method using rotting manure in 400 B.C. Several records exist of high-born Roman ladies foretelling the sex of their offspring by hatching an egg tucked under their breasts.

Numerous descriptions of methods using the heat of the human body are recorded throughout history and from all over the world. Philippine islanders paid their servants to lie on eggs. The eggs were laid between rows of sticks on a bed of ashes, and both servant and eggs were covered with blankets. South African farmers employed native girls to hatch ostrich eggs with body heat, when the feathers of these birds were in terrific demand.

Mechanical hatching did not come to the Western world until 1749, when Réamur in Paris developed the first mechanical box to hatch eggs. He used the ether capsule as a thermostat. In 1770, Campion was successful using a special room heated by the flues of his boiler.

The first successful commercial machine was the hot water incubator made by Hearson in 1881, and in 1895 Cypher put his 20,000 duck egg model on the market. The first all-electric automated machine did not appear until 1922.

PARAFFIN STILL-AIR INCUBATORS

These were the first machines to be commercially produced. In the hands of an artist they were, and still are, quite capable of producing superb hatches. Many are still used today as hatchers in game farms. Handling them is an art, not a science.

Still-air is really a misnomer, for the air is not still at all, but moving under convection. They should really be called convection incubators. The original models were heated by paraffin. The flame from the burning wick is outside the incubator, at the base of a short chimney. There are two outlets at the top of the chimney, one with a damper on it opening straight into the room, and the other running at right angles into the top of the incubator. Raising the damper allows all the heat to escape into the room, while lowering it diverts all the hot air into the top of the incubator. The damper is raised and lowered by the expansion and contraction of an ether capsule, which works a series of levers.

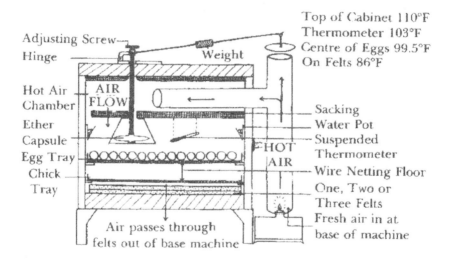

Fig. 9.1. Paraffin still-air incubator

The hot air chamber and the flue leading into it are so designed and insulated that it has an even temperature throughout. The hot air escapes down into the egg chamber through a sacking partition.

The egg chamber is not at the same temperature throughout. The top is 10-20°F (5.5-11°C) hotter than the bottom. Only at one level will the temperature be correct for hatching; above this it will be too hot, and below it too cool. The egg tray and thermometer must be at the right level.

Temperature control

First, the thermometer is correctly sited above the eggs. The flame is then adjusted so that it supplies only fractionally more heat than is required with the damper fully shut. With the weight in the middle of the lever arm to the damper, the adjusting screw is turned so that the damper is raised off the chimney ¼ inch. Minor adjustments are made by sliding the damper up and down the lever arm. If the weight is too near the hinge and adjusting screw, the damper will move about too much, giving very uneven control. If it is too near the damper, the pressure on the capsule will render it sluggish and insensitive.

These machines will only work satisfactorily if they are absolutely level, and the temperature of the incubator room maintained at a constant day and night temperature of about 60°F (15.5°C).

Continual adjustments of the controls are necessary, as the wick needs trimming daily, and the ether capsule responds to changes in barometric pressure as well as temperature. Variations of up to 5°F (2.7°C) can be caused by changes in the weather, although the presence of the weight on the damper arm tends to minimize this.

Another troublesome cause of temperature variation is the metal rod connecting the capsule to the outside lever. Looseness of this rod in the sockets at each end can cause it to move and alter the friction as it passes through the various holes in its path.

The temperature is also controlled by the presence or absence of felts in the floor of the machine that obstruct the flow of hot air out through the bottom of the egg chamber. Increasing the air-flow lowers the temperature of both the floor and the egg tray. Most machines have three felts in the bottom, more if the machine is sited in a cold room, and one is removed at roughly weekly intervals. This compensates for the generative heat of the eggs as they develop, as well as providing them with the necessary increased ventilation.

Humidity control

This is just as much an art as temperature control. There are water trays in the machine, but it is usually necessary to maintain high humidity in the incubator room by frequently dampening, or washing, the floor of the room, or even by maintaining containers of damp peat under the ventilation windows. The more sophisticated, later models incorporate a drip feed of water into the chimney. Spraying the eggs with warm water is often necessary.

Turning
Turning is usually done by hand.

ELECTRIC STILL-AIR INCUBATORS

Replacing the oil flame by an electric element is simple enough, and many of the original paraffin models are still going strong after being converted. Conversion to electricity, however, slightly alters the characteristics of the machine, and many conversions seem unsuccessful because of this.

The burning oil produces carbon dioxide and water. This is fed directly into the incubator as the flue gases. Heating air by an electric element does not produce any carbon dioxide and has the effect of lowering the relative humidity of the air being heated. Carbon dioxide must be added to the machine by lowering the ventilation rate, and the humidity of either the room or the machine must be increased substantially.

The advent of the microswitch made it possible to put the heaters inside the incubator, regulating the temperature by switching them on and off.

THERMOSTATS

The thermostat is the most vital part of any incubator. Humidity, ventilation and turning of the eggs can all be done routinely by the operator, but he cannot maintain a continuous watch on his eggs, turning the heaters on and off every few minutes. A sensitive and reliable thermostat is essential.

Many of the smaller incubators still rely on the ether capsule, though this has long been abandoned by the manufacturers of larger machines as being too variable in its control, and too prone to develop faults to give reliable operation.

The ether capsule
In essence, the ether capsule is a small quantity of liquid ether enclosed in a metal envelope. This is usually made from two small sheets of flexible metal that have been soldered together at the edges. On warming, the ether expands, enlarging the space between

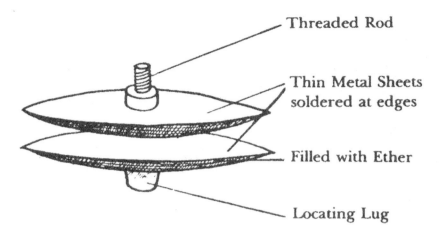

Threaded Rod

Thin Metal Sheets
soldered at edges

Filled with Ether

Locating Lug

Fig.9.2. Double ether capsule

the metal sheets with sufficient force to operate the mechanism. At room temperature the ether is liquid, but becomes gas at incubation temperatures. Unless this ether gas is under some pressure in the capsule, it will also expand and contract with changes of atmospheric pressure, necessitating constant readjustment of the controls. Too much pressure renders it insensitive. A single ether capsule working directly on the micro-switch is often supplied with the smaller, cheaper machines, but is not really sensitive enough. Sensitivity can be increased by using two or three capsules joined together, or by making the capsule operate levers.

The mercury switch
   Some machines use a capsule to operate a mercury switch. This is a short length of sealed glass tube containing a bead of mercury in a vacuum. The contact wires are sealed into the glass so that they do not quite touch. Tilting the switch rolls the bead of mercury down the tube, so that it touches both contact wires and completes the circuit. To be sensitive, these switches can take only a limited electric current, so they can only be used for relatively small heaters.

Fig. 9.3. A.B. Multilife 600, fully automatic, general purpose setter

The mercury contact thermometer

The expansion of a liquid as it is warmed is the principle of all mercury thermometers. A fairly large bulk of mercury is held in a glass bulb, with the expansion occurring into a fine capillary tube. Small changes of temperature will give large movements of mercury up and down the capillary tube.

If two fine wires are inserted into this capillary tube, one in permanent contact with the mercury and the other at the level the mercury column will reach at a predetermined temperature, these wire contacts can be used to complete an electrical circuit when this temperature is reached.

However, as the current will only flow when above this temperature, and the thermometer can only take small, low voltage currents, it cannot be used to switch the current directly to the heaters. It can, however, activate a relay that switches the heaters off. As the temperature falls, the mercury leaving the contact wire breaks the circuit to the relay, and the heaters come on again. This circuit of transformer, contact thermometer, and relay switch is commonly used in large commercial incubators.

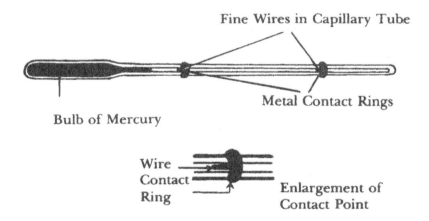

Fig. 9.4. Mercury contact thermometer

Every electrical or mechanical device must have a failure rate, even if these failures are infrequent. As can be seen from the circuit diagram, any poor connection or fault in the circuit will leave the heaters on.

In the warm moist air of the incubator corrosion of the metal contacts of the thermometer is a common cause of overheating.

The continual operation of the contact points of the main relays causes them to wear, so that the current to the heaters arcs across them. This arcing acts like an electric welder, and worn points can fuse together, another relatively common cause of incubator overheating. Most incubators utilising the contact thermometer principle are usually also fitted with overheating alarms, and a safety ether capsule and microswitch. Many are fitted with spark suppressors.

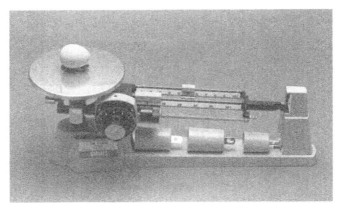

Triple Beam Balance

Digital Balance
Fig. 9.5. Egg weighing balances

Solid State Electronic Temperature Sensing and Switching
Any metal clashing against metal, as in a switch, has a high inbuilt failure rate. The failure rate of solid state devices is significantly lower, and most of the large commercial machines are now fitted with these solid state switches. They come in many sizes, shapes and capacities, but all are capable of switching on and off at fifty times per second (i.e. mains frequency) without detriment.

Whether you are using Density loss techniques or the more commonly used Weight loss techniques, you will need to start your eggs off in a particular humidity.

If you have kept good records from last year then you will not have a problem. If fact if you have kept records for each egg then you will know if any particular pair of birds throw odd eggs that need a strange humidity.

If you are not sure what humidity to use, it is suggested that you start at 55% Relative Humidity. On a wet bulb reading this would be 84°F presuming that you are incubating at 99.5°F or 37.5°C dry bulb.

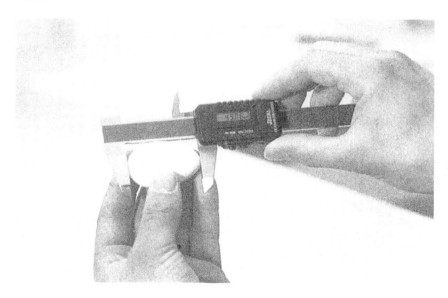

Fig. 9.6. Measuring an egg for density

155

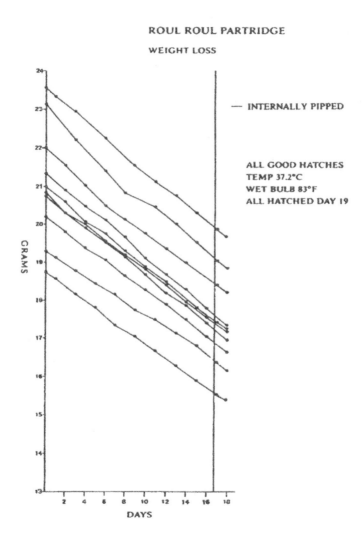

Fig. 9.7. Weight loss graph of roulroul partridge eggs
This graph shows the weight loss of 10 Roulroul
partridge eggs against the days of incubation

If you are incubating large numbers of common pheasant or partridge eggs then this sort of humidity level will be fine until they start to pip, when maximum humidity will be required.

For converting fahrenheit temperatures to centigrade, refer to *Appendix 1.*

To work out your relative humidity refer to *Appendix 1*

The following are some guidelines for specific species but please remember these are averages and individual eggs can vary immensely.

Species	Wet Bulb	Rel. Hum.	Species	Wet Bulb	Rel. Hum.
Pheasants	84°F	55%	Spoonbills	70°F	24%
Partridge	84°F	55%	Guineafowl	84°F	55%
Parrots	80 - 84°F	45 - 55%	Cranes	84°F	55%
Waterfowl	84°F	55%	Rollers	78°F	42%
Penguins	75°F	34%	Kookaburras	80°F	45%
Ostrich	70°F	24%	Oystercatcher	80°F	45%
Rhea	80°F	45%	Touraco	84°F	55%

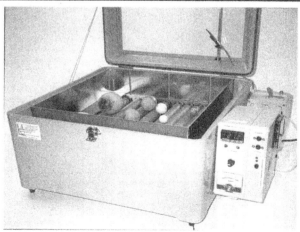

Fig. 9.8. A.B.Newlife Mk6 fully automatic incubator, with variable turning rollers

Incubator hatching

OSTRICH

EGG No.	WEIGHT LOSS	SHELL THICKNESS	TEMP.	HUMIDITY
286	17.3%	2.01 mm	36.2 °C	OFF
246	19.6%	1.8 mm	36.2 °C	OFF
236	17%	1.82 mm	36.2 °C	OFF

TURNING: BY HAND SEVEN TIMES A DAY.

DAY 40 IS TWO DAYS
BEFORE HATCH

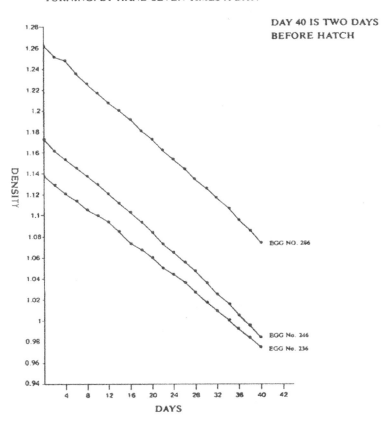

Fig. 9.9. This graph shows the density loss of three ostrich eggs
against the days of incubation

158

HEATING ELEMENTS

All heating elements consist of a length of resistance wire that gives out heat as a current passes through it. Some are bare, some protected by a silicate tube, and some enclosed in an earthed metal sheath filled with inert insulating powder. The heat given out is measured in watts.

The size and positioning of the heaters is a critical factor in any incubator design. Still-air machines have low wattage heaters widely distributed to give an even heat, while fan assisted machines depend on air movement to distribute the heat from a smaller, more powerful source.

Hysteresis

The sensitivity of temperature control depends not only on the inherent sensitivity of the thermostat, but a combination of other factors. How long it takes the sensing device to respond, plus the distance of this sensing device from the heaters with the time it takes for the heat to reach the sensor, as well as the output of the heaters relative to the size of the incubator box.

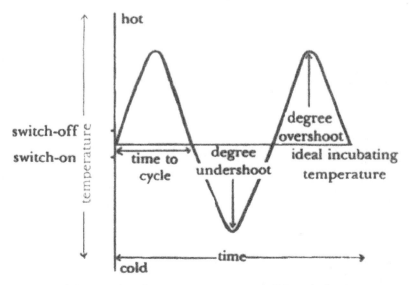

Fig. 9.10. Effect on incubator temperature of delays in heater response to thermostat action

In any incubator there will be an inevitable time lag between the thermostat calling for heat and the heaters supplying it. Equally, when the heaters are switched off, they take a finite time to cool, giving a degree of overshoot.

The bulky ether capsules and relatively large heaters of some of the smaller still-air table models can give temperature fluctuations of almost 10°F (5.5°C) between switch on and switch off, particularly if they have just been opened. This is not good for the eggs.

The nearer the thermostat is to the heaters, the quicker it will respond. This will give superb temperature control around the heaters, but if the eggs are placed some distance away and the insulation of the machine is not one hundred per cent, the egg temperature can fluctuate markedly with the room temperature. If the thermostat is among the eggs, the thermal delay can cause wide temperature over- and under-shoots.

HUMIDITY CONTROL IN ELECTRIC INCUBATORS

All incubators need added water and there are numerous methods of supplying the correct amount.* Altering the size of the water pots will alter the surface area of water exposed and hence the humidity. Filling the same water trays at definite intervals and then allowing them to dry out achieves the same result.

Water trays with a sloping base will give a larger surface area when full. The surface area can be altered by the level of water in the tray, which can be kept constant by a simple inverted bottle with a spout. Water can only come out of the spout when the level in the tray drops sufficiently to allow air into the bottle. As soon as the desired level is reached, no further water can be added.

Although humidity control by the size of the area of water exposed is cheap and easy, it takes no account of the prevailing humidity of the atmosphere, which can profoundly affect the relative humidity in the incubator. Constant monitoring of the weather, the eggs, and the size of water pot is essential for good results. Many of the good and bad breeding seasons can be directly attributed to the natural humidity of

* we now know some species need very dry conditions in which to artificially incubate their eggs and therefore no humidity is required; de-humidifiers are sometimes needed to reduce the ambient humidity in the incubation room at some locations.

the air, although the levels in the water containers were maintained correctly. The correct relative humidity can only be maintained if it is accurately measured and water added in response to this measurement

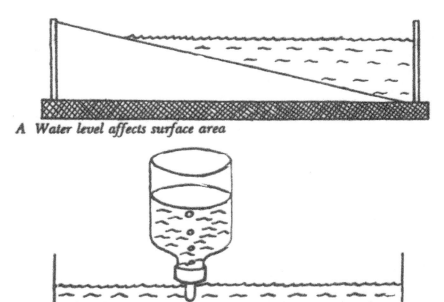

A Water level affects surface area

B Constant water level device

Fig. 9.11. Humidity control using sloping water traps

Measuring relative humidity
The hair hygrometers and colour change hygrometers will give an indication if the incubator is too wet or too dry, but they are not sufficiently accurate to give other than a general guide to conditions, unless one of the very expensive models is acquired. Since the response time to change is of the order of half an hour, they cannot be used to control the input of water to a machine.

Bulb surrounded by wet wick

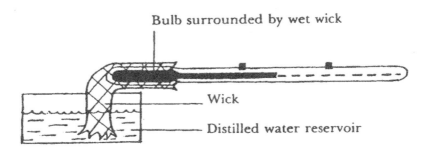

Fig. 9.12.Humidity control by the wet bulb method

Recent developments have allowed the possibility of purchasing a humidity controller to convert older machines with unsophisticated humidity control. The humidity controller from A.B. Incubators has been based on the successful fully automatic electronic device fitted as standard on all their incubators. This unit is now housed within its own cabinet and can be used with most makes of incubators that have wet -bulb facilities. (The most recent model no longer uses a wet-bulb system; a solid-state humidity sensor provides the switching for the water flow into the machine, up to a predetermined set humidity.)

This unique device, using the latest solid state components, has been developed for use with any existing incubator with a capacity of 1200 eggs or less.

The new generation of electronic sensors are very promising but not as expensive as in the past and are now in general use.

A practical, inexpensive, and reliable method is to use the wet Bulb principle, either on a mercury thermometer or on an electronic sensor bead, as illustrated in Figure 9.12.

The water can be supplied to the incubator either as a fine spray jet into the air flow, or as a slow drip into an evaporation area. A solenoid valve is used to control the flow of water.

The solenoid valve works on exactly the same principle as the heater relay, except that the soft iron core, which becomes magnetised when the coil is energised, is enclosed in a watertight brass tube. A rubber plug in its lower end either stops or permits, the flow of water through the tube, in response to the controls.

TURNING MECHANISMS

Hand turning

This is the oldest and simplest method. Every egg is marked on one side with an X and on the other with an 0, to ensure that no egg remains unturned. Turning every egg by hand several times a day can become a tedious chore if there are more than a few eggs. Failure to turn for even one day can have dire consequences at hatching time.

Hand-operated turning

There are several ingenious methods of turning many eggs at once. Two are illustrated in the diagram. (Figure 9.13).

1. The eggs are laid on their sides resting on roller bars which sit on a wooden runner, so that pushing or pulling the entire roller tray rotates the eggs. Each roller tray is designed for a particular size of egg.

2. The eggs lie on their sides in rows on a wire mesh tray. A movable wire rod frame, with a simple push-pull device, rolls the eggs over each time it is operated. Each tray, with its wire rods, can take only one size of egg.

If the egg is set vertically, tilting it over 45° to the vertical will effectively put one surface on top. Returning it to the vertical, and then tilting it 45° in the opposite direction, will effectively turn it over (Figure 9.14).

The same result can be achieved, with less jolting to the eggs, if they are packed together, small end down, and the whole tray rotated through 45°.

Automatic turning

The parent bird has been shown to turn its eggs about every thirty-five minutes. Large scale chicken producers, have found that hourly turning produces the optimum results; to turn by hand at these frequencies is obviously impossible. All the large incubators using automatic turning use the tilting tray principle.

In incubators holding a thousand eggs or less, the egg trays slide into a rigid cradle, and the whole cradle rotates backwards and forwards on a central spindle. Rotation is achieved by means of an electric motor, suitably geared down, and connected to the central

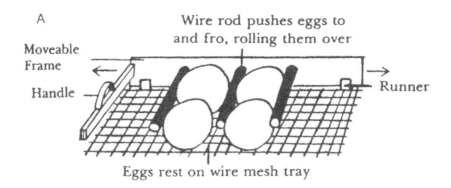

A

Wire rod pushes eggs to
and fro, rolling them over

Moveable
Frame

Handle

Runner

Eggs rest on wire mesh tray

B

Fig. 9.13. A   Hand-operated turning
           B   Eggs resting on rollers. Pushing or pulling entire
                roller tray rotates eggs

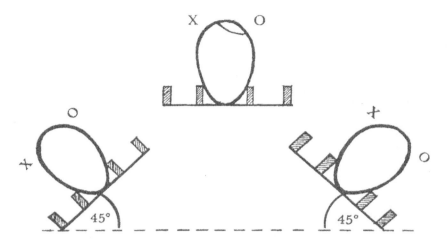

Fig. 9.14. Turning effect of setting eggs vertically

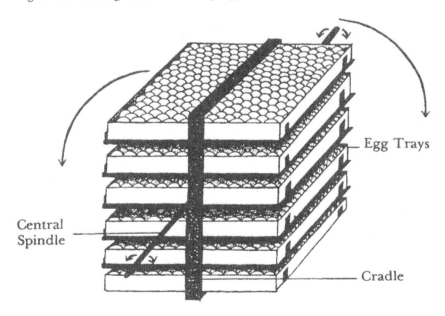

Fig. 9.15. Automatic turning of egg trays

Fig. 9.16. Partridge egg storage trolleys

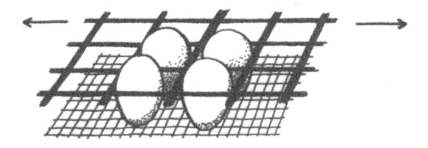

Fig. 9.17. Further method of hand-operated turning
The eggs sit on a wire mesh, small end down, and the grid is moved
forwards and backwards

Fig. 9.18. Variable roller turning in the A.B.Newlife 75 Mk 6 incubator

spindle either with camshafts or a belt and pulley. A time clock initiates the turning, and limit switches turn off the motor when the desired angle of tilt has been reached.

In incubators holding thousands of eggs, the rows of trays are in pairs, and the cradles are not rigid but hinged. Up and down movement of a central rod tilts the trays. Control is by a similar time clock and limits switch. The central rod is usually moved by a rack and pinion, whole banks of trays being connected to one large geared motor and a common shaft.

VENTILATION

The air-flow over the eggs is the critical factor in incubation design. In still-air machines, the air moves by convection. Even distribution of heat is achieved in some small table models by the addition of a fan.

In cabinet incubators fans are essential if large numbers of eggs are to be incubated simultaneously, as they accommodate more than one row of eggs and the whole cabinet is to be maintained at the same temperature. The air is moved round by fans or paddles, and turning is either automatic or mechanical

Fig. 9.19. Marcon Gamestock RS 20,000 fully automatic game setter

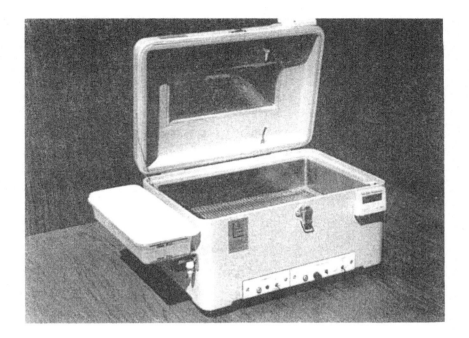

Fig. 9.20. A.B.Startlife 25 reptile incubator

Large scale incubation, involving hundreds of thousands of eggs weekly, is now done in walk-in machines, where the entire room is maintained at incubation environment. Heavy plastic curtains hang beside the banks of eggs, directing the air flow from ducts in the ceiling. Preconditioning chambers warm and moisten the air before it reaches the eggs. Part of the air is re-circulated and part is passed out of exhaust vents.

Chapter 10

INCUBATION TECHNIQUES

THE INCUBATOR ROOM

The environment in an incubator room is almost as important as the environment within the incubator itself. It is much easier to maintain a constant environment in a brick building with good insulation than it is in a small draughty wooden shed. Accordingly, the reader is advised to use an incubation room that keeps at a steady temperature at all times.

Temperature

An even temperature of 60 - 70°F (15.5 – 21.1°C) is essential. The fluctuations between day and night temperatures can be easily checked with a greenhouse maximum and minimum thermometer, and if this exceeds more than 10°F (5.5°C), the insulation of the room should be increased, or the room provided with a thermostatically controlled heater. In the event of the temperature rising above 70°F (21.1°C), an extractor fan is more than useful. Dampening the floor will rapidly lower the room temperature, besides increasing the humidity. Records of the daily maximum and minimum temperatures should be kept as a routine.

Humidity

As far as is possible the humidity of the room should be kept constant. In those machines with automatic humidity supply controlled by a wet bulb sensing device in the machine, any variation in atmospheric humidity is automatically corrected within the machine. In those incubators that are not automatic the humidity will mirror the atmospheric humidity. The constant area of evaporating water in the incubator will give out a constant increase of water in the machine, but this will not always be the correct amount.

The natural moisture in the air will be much greater in the bottom of a damp valley than it will be on the top of a hill. In the early spring the natural moisture is much greater than it is in mid-summer. A simple hygrometer for the incubator room will give sufficient indication of the relative humidity to help decide whether to add more water or not.

Ventilation
Ventilation is essential, particularly if large numbers of eggs are being incubated. The machines take in their fresh air from the room, and give out their stale air. If the room feels at all stuffy, it could be affecting the eggs.

Sunlight must not be allowed to fall on the machines, for in a very short space of time it can overheat them. It is always better to fit windows and ventilation ducts on the north side of the building if possible.

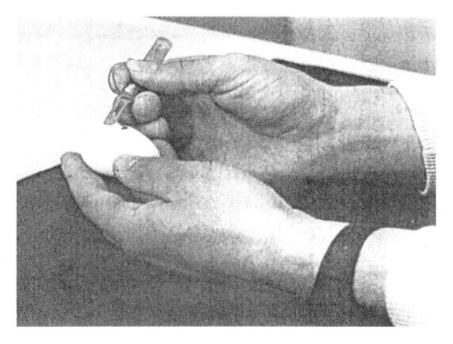

Fig. 10.1. Dirt removal prior to washing

Hygiene

Dirt carries disease. The incubator room should be kept as clean as a baby's nursery, for after all, that is what it is. Introduced into an incubator, one germ can become a million overnight. They can come in on dirty eggs, buckets, hands, or the clothing of the operator. Rats, mice, flies, cockroaches, etc. are all spreaders of disease and should not be tolerated.

The incubator room is often regarded as a convenient place to put dead or diseased birds, and all sorts of other unsavoury items. This is not a good practice. The incubator room should be reserved for nothing but incubation. If only one small machine is being used, it is far better to suffer domestic disharmony by keeping it in the kitchen than risk poor hatches by having it in the garden shed.

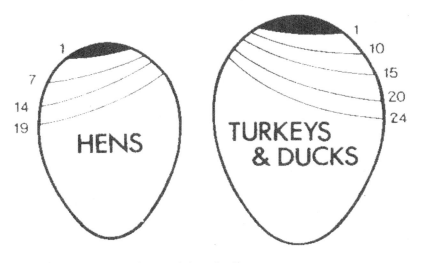

Number indicates days of incubation

Fig. 10.2. Air cell sizes in hen, turkeys and ducks

One of the first machines the author made produced spectacular hatches in the 1976 season, housed in a wooden shed with no door, in the shade of a very large tree. That year was very hot and sunny. In the following year, which was extremely cold and wet, the hatches were disastrous. They did not improve until the machine was moved into a special room in an old brick building with a thatched roof.

Two of these machines, working at the Wildfowl Trust at Slimbridge, were found not to use any water at all. The humidity in the incubator room was sufficiently high, due to the presence of all the hatchers and the routine washing of the floor.

PRE-INCUBATION CARE OF THE EGGS

The care given to the eggs before they go into the incubator can decide whether or not they hatch. It is one of the key factors in successful incubation. Many of the late death embryos in incubators can be directly attributed to mismanagement before the egg was set.

Collecting the eggs

The eggs of all domestic birds, pheasants, and quail should be gathered as soon as possible after laying, as they will continue to lay regardless. Waterfowl are more of a problem, as too much disturbance will put them off. If the nest is obviously safe, it is better to collect the completed clutch; if not, daily collection and replacement by dummies is advisable.

The quicker an egg is cooled to storage temperature, the better it will keep. Eggs left lying in the sun will start to develop slowly, which can weaken or kill them later. Temporary chilling, even to near freezing point, is not over-harmful, provided that the egg does not actually freeze and crack, but prolonged cold is detrimental.

Cleaning the eggs

Nest clean eggs should be collected in a different container from the dirty ones and, if possible, stored separately. Many large commercial concerns will not set dirty eggs at all because of their lower hatchability, and because of the increased liability of contamination of the incubators from "bangers" and rotten eggs. Clean eggs may be put straight into the store, but in any case should be handled separately.

The dirty ones should be dry cleaned with sandpaper, and then washed in a detergent disinfectant. The manufacturer's instructions on time, temperature, and concentration must be followed exactly. After drying naturally on a wire rack, they may join their fellows in the store.

Pre-incubation sterilisation
It is arguable whether further sterilisation of the shell is advisable before storage, but all large chicken hatcheries routinely dip their eggs at this stage. Most game farmers wash and sterilise only dirty pheasant eggs, but routinely treat all duck eggs with a detergent disinfectant dip or wash.

Storage
No egg should be kept longer than a week before setting. To store at all in an incubator room kept at 70°F (21 1°C) for the incubators is asking for trouble. The construction of a proper egg store will pay for itself in the first season. This should be kept at 55°F (12.7°C) and 70% relative humidity. The bottom half of an old domestic refrigerator is better than nothing. If adequate storage facilities are not available, it is far wiser not to store at all and have problems rearing the chicks hatched in dribbles, than go to all the trouble of producing and incubating an egg for no purpose.

Setting the eggs
No matter what make of incubator is used, it should give a reasonable hatch if set up properly in the correct conditions. The eggs should be allowed to warm up to room temperature slowly, preferably overnight, before being set. The manufacturer's instructions on temperature, humidity, ventilation holes, or the number and site of felts, insulating materials, etc. must be followed to the letter
It is not a good idea to mix together eggs of different sizes and ages of incubation in machines that have only one tray, as they can adversely affect each other. In cabinet machines, with several trays, any instructions about where to place fresh eggs and when to move trays must be complied with exactly. In the mad rush of the breeding season, eggs often get put wherever there is a space, but it is better to keep together all eggs due to hatch about the same time. Mixing species such as geese and pheasants in the same tray, especially if this is a small machine with only one layer of eggs, usually results in a bad hatch of both. Not only do the eggs need different temperature, humidity and ventilation settings, but also eggs massed in an incubator tend to create their own environment. This can generate hot spots over the large eggs, which affect the thermostat

Fig.10.3. Setting partridge eggs in a Marcon Gamestock RS20000
Setter

and cause temperature fluctuations. Waterfowl eggs are notorious carriers of bacteria that can be lethal to such eggs as pheasants.

Where incubators are only used as a result of a shortage of broody hens, the hens should have the eggs first. A good broody hen will beat most incubators in the first week. The eggs should be candled before transfer, and then trayed up in the normal manner without chilling them.

Where eggs are packed in trays point down, packing is

enormously facilitated if one end of the tray is raised. Batches and species can be separated by a rigid partition of polystyrene, or a book end piece of wood.

MONITORING PROGRESS

A daily chart should be kept of the incubator room maximum and minimum temperatures and humidity. A record of the thermometer readings in the incubators should also be kept, particularly if control is by ether capsule and subject to atmospheric pressure variations. The readings of any hygrometer in the incubator should be noted and, if turning is not automatic, this should be recorded each time too.

If these records are accurately kept, many of the previously unexplained poor hatches will have an obvious explanation, and preventative measures can be taken to stop it happening again.

Candling the eggs

The contents of a fresh egg will permit light to pass through it. Any embryonic development will show up as darker material. The term 'candling' is obviously very old, from the days when the only known light source was a candle. It is surprising how much can be seen in a dark room with the egg held just in front of a candle.

Many of the leading aviculturists who hatch entirely by broody hen can candle eggs very accurately using only the light from a dusty window. The technique is very simple and, once acquired, very useful for checking parent-incubated eggs without moving them far from the nest. The egg is held between the little finger and the palm of the left hand, and the right hand cups round the finger and the egg. If the egg is now held up to one eye, the only light coming to the eye is through the egg. The trick is not to look at the egg, but to hold the egg very close to the eye, staring into the distance through it. Although out of focus, it is easy to see the size of the air cell, the degree of development, and the telltale signs of death, especially if the egg is pointed at the sun.

Fig. 10.4. Candling appearance of eggs during incubation
(see over page on pages 178 & 179)
a. **48 hours**. *The blastodisc can be clearly seen*
b. **Third day**. *The yolk sac blood vessels developed*
c. **Fifth day**. *Considerable growth of the embryo*
d. **Seventh day**. *Movement of the embryo during the time of exposure makes it appear larger than it really is*
e. **Twelfth day**. *Greater exposure to show the increasing size of the air cell, and the unabsorbed albumen in the small end of the egg*
f. **Sixteenth day**. *Residual pockets of albumen almost totally enclosed. When the large allantoic vein shuts off, the air cell will suddenly become much larger*
g. **Sixteenth day**. *This egg, though alive, will not hatch. The air space is too small, and the membranes are stunted, as shown by the sharp edge, and there is no network of small blood vessels*
h. **Sixteenth day and onwards**. *Fully blacked out with nice sharp demarcation between the air cell and embryo, and no residual albumen visible*

Fig. 10.5. Enlarged details of the daily development of the chicken embryo over its 21 day incubation period
(Pages 180 - 182)
This fine set of photographs comes from the
TAD PHARMAZEUTISCHES WERK GMBH Poster
P.O. Box 720 .2190 Cuxhaven. Germany

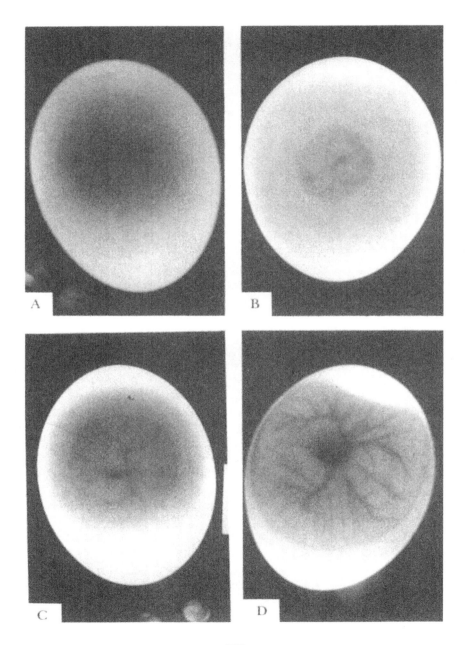

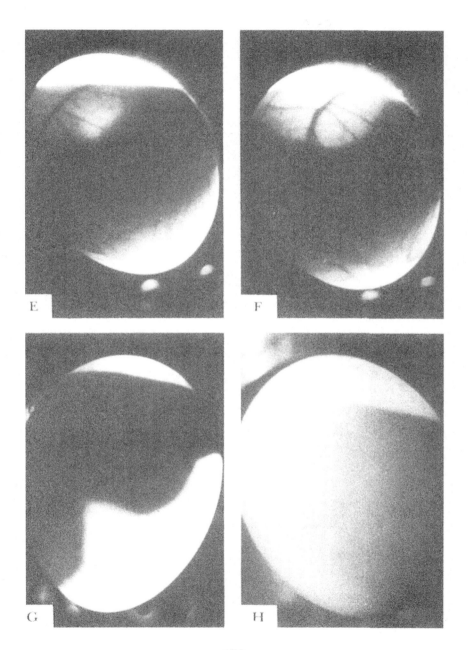

DAY

2

4

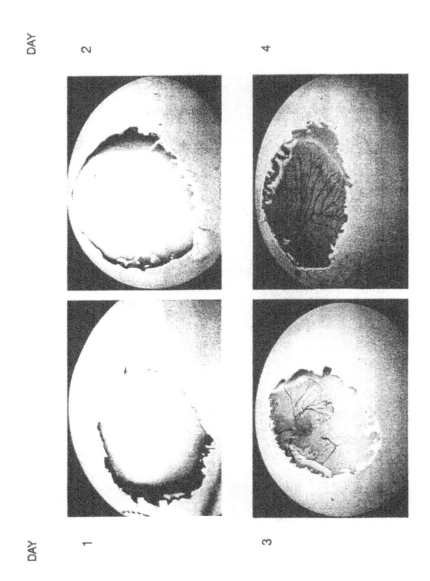

DAY

1

3

DAY

DAY

5

6

9

10

13

14

17

18

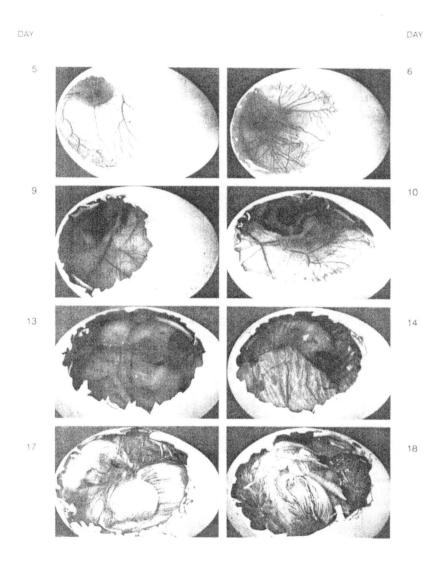

7

8

11

12

15

16

19

20

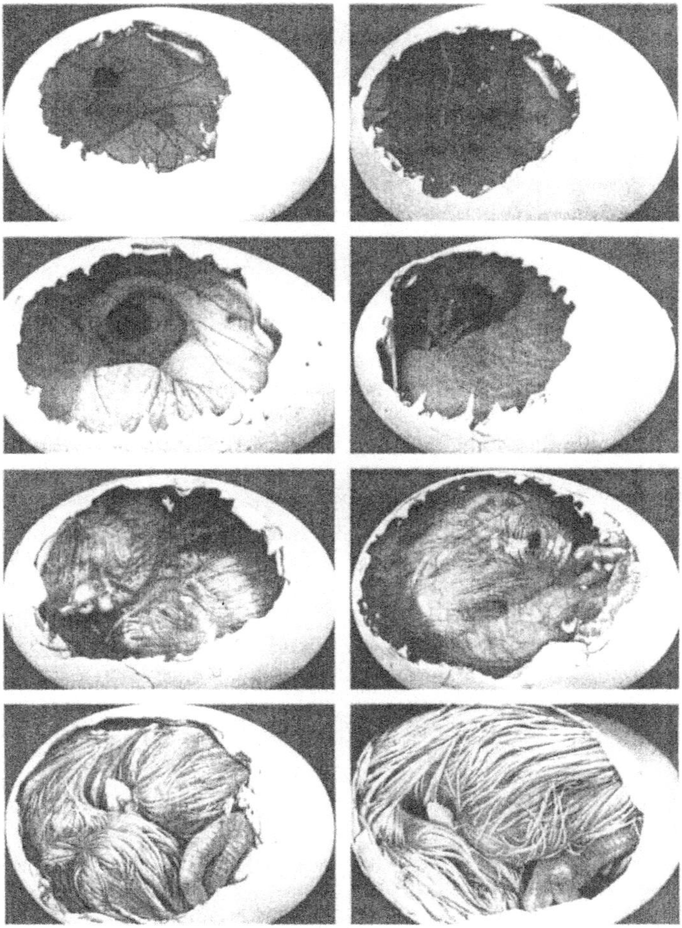

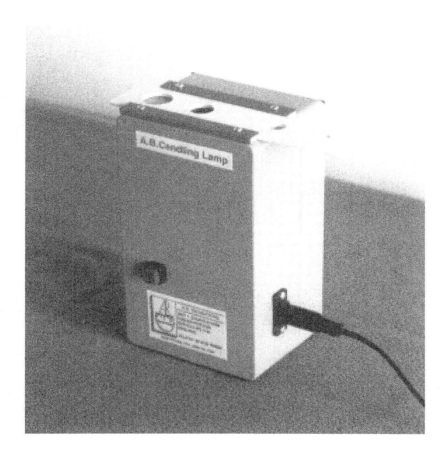

Fig.10.6. A.B.Tungsten Halogen Egg Candling Lamp

Candling lamps are many and varied. They can be made from powerful torches or use normal light bulbs. However, the Tungsten Halogen dicronic lamp illustrated above has a special reflector which disperse the heat produced by the lamp in the opposite direction to the light beams, lying very low forward infra-red emission, allowing the lamp to be used to illuminate delicate eggs without risk of damage by heat. A slide with various holes restricts to light to egg size to be candled.

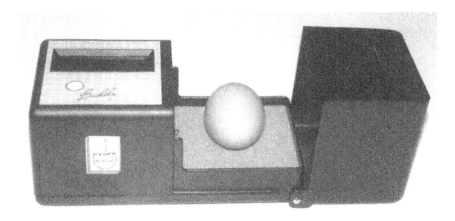

Fig.10.7. "Buddy " Infra-red Candling Lamp

The majority of eggs have white or light coloured shells which allow a powerful light to show embryo development, but there are other species where the egg shells are thick or densely coloured and will not allow a light to show through them. The latest development is an infra-red lamp which projects a beam through the shell of the egg and detects any movement in the egg, whether it be blood pumping through the veins or the embryo itself. A digital read-out on a screen shows movement, indicating that the embryo is alive.

Positive movement can be detected approx 5 days into incubation. Being battery operated, the lamp can be taken into the field to candle eggs.

Commercially made candlers have a rim of rubber round the hole. Besides making a light-tight seal with the egg, it also prevents accidental damage.

The more powerful the light, the more clearly will the contents be seen, but too powerful a bulb gives out too much heat. Not only can this damage the egg, it can also give the operator a nasty burn on the fingers. A forty watt bulb placed about 1/4 inch from the egg gives very adequate viewing. A handy switch that will turn off the light between eggs will prevent the candler overheating.

It is possible to candle eggs without removing them from the egg trays by mounting an enclosed light bulb on a short handle and moving it over the eggs. Clears and deaths are marked with a pencil and removed afterwards. Where thousands of eggs are candled at one session, a strip light mounted under a slot in a table surface permits a whole row of eggs to be seen at once. The finest candling light is ultraviolet. Dark glasses, with a powerful ultraviolet light filter, must be worn when using this, for it can permanently damage the eyes. It is especially useful for pheasants and other eggs where the thick, pigmented shell obscures the view. (Check with your local Health & Safety department that you are permitted to use this type of candling). Some of the larger game farmers candle a whole tray of eggs at once by placing the tray over a tray-size light.

The purpose of candling is to eliminate infertile, dead, or damaged eggs. It is also an integral part of humidity control to check the air cell sizes. All eggs should be candled routinely once a week. The removal of dead eggs will considerably increase the chances of the others of hatching.

The size of the air cell is one of the major yardsticks for assessing the progress of incubation. Many species of birds have thick shells that appear granular through the candler, and are often heavily pigmented as well. Without a powerful light, the size of the air cell is all that can be seen clearly in the early stages. After half the incubation period, the clears can be distinguished from those that have 'blacked out'.

If the air cell is too large, the humidity level should be raised, either to the room or to the incubator. If it is too small, the humidity level should be reduced, either by increasing the ventilation through the machine or by lessening the surface area of evaporating water in the machine. In small table machines the only practical way of increasing the humidity for waterfowl eggs is to spray the eggs with warm water once a day. A very common cause of failure to hatch in pheasant eggs is too much water in the early stages. Weekly monitoring of the air cell size will allow corrections to be made.

Weekly candling, besides being very informative, can also have other benefits. Among several dozens of supposedly mallard eggs that were being incubated, the author noted that there were several eggs whose air cell size and general rate of development was significantly behind the others. By the time of the third candling, when the mallard were obviously near to hatching, these eggs were far from it. They were separated from the mallard, and on the thirtieth day hatched into a splendid clutch of European Goldeneye. Had their progress not been monitored, all would have been thrown out on the twenty-eighth day as dead in shell mallard.

Humidity control

Judging air cell size is an art. Many of the old gamekeepers make very accurate assessments of humidity need and progress of incubation by using the methods perfected by the ancient Egyptians. The feel and sound of two eggs rolled together in one hand is quite different when the eggs are fresh from that of eggs near to hatching. The well-incubated eggs are lighter and emit a more hollow noise as they clink together. Another old trick is to put the eggs in a bucket of warm water. A fresh egg will sink and one with an air cell will float. Movement of the chick within the egg will cause it to bob about on the surface of the water. Absence of movement is taken as an indication of death.

The most accurate method of actually measuring the humidity requirements of an egg, as opposed to estimating it, is to weigh it at periodic intervals and plot a simple graph of the weight loss. In order to hatch, an egg must lose about 15% of its initial weight by hatching time. There is an exact mathematical relationship between the porosity of the shell, the length of the incubation period, and the relative humidity needed to hatch the egg. If the porosity of the shell is known, it is quite simple to calculate the necessary humidity needed to hatch the egg, and to predict the weight loss under a given humidity.

Unfortunately, even in such a standardised bird as the domestic hen, the porosity of eggs laid at the beginning of the season is less than those laid towards the end, so that although theoretically one can predict the humidity required for any species. In practice it is still necessary to measure the effects on the egg to check that the calculation was right.

For all practical purposes, the graph of optimum weight loss can be regarded as a straight line; all species must lose 6% by the half way stage, and 12% by internal pip.

Most of the weighing scales available are not sufficiently accurate to measure 6% of a pheasant or quail egg, but they are accurate enough to measure 6% of ten, or even a hundred eggs, so that it is probably better to weigh a batch of eggs and calculate the average weight. Weighing the whole clutch, or a sample of larger numbers, and then calculating the average will remove the complications of infertile and dead eggs among the ones initially weighed. For smaller eggs, where accurate weight loss is required, there are scales now available that will weight to an accuracy of 0.001gm, but they are expensive.

Although it sounds very troublesome, in fact it is not. A pencil, graph paper, and a set of reasonably accurate kitchen scales are all the equipment needed, and if all the measurements are made in grams, the mathematics is very simple.

HATCHING

Where large numbers of a single species of egg are being hatched, it is usual to transfer them to the hatchers on a specified day, usually two days before the anticipated hatch. Where there is a medley of assorted species and the exact hatching date is not specifically known, eggs should not be transferred until all the clutch is in the air cell or the first few eggs actually chipped. It is an undoubted fact that the embryo pierces the membranes into the air space more easily in a dry shell atmosphere. During the period that this is happening, a low humidity will increase the hatch. Where the setting period and hatching are done in the same machine, it is very important to refill the water pots so that their empty period coincides with this period in the development of the egg. As soon as roughly one third of the eggs are chipped, the humidity should be raised to its maximum. Many hatches are ruined by the operator opening the door to see how things are progressing, thus allowing all the warm and moist air in the hatcher to escape. After the door has been shut again, the heaters soon restore the temperature, but it can take up to half an hour to restore the humidity. During this time, the exposed membranes of the hatching eggs dry out and prevent an otherwise perfect chick emerging successfully.

The membranes of pheasant eggs become very tough with even the slightest drop in humidity, and the exhausted chick may not have the strength to break them. For this reason, many game farmers find that they cannot hatch in moving air, and do all their hatching in still-air machines. Pheasant eggs will hatch perfectly well in moving air, provided that they first have the dry shell period while the chicks are breaking into the air spaces, and then have the humidity raised to nearly 85%, and maintained there until all the chicks are out.

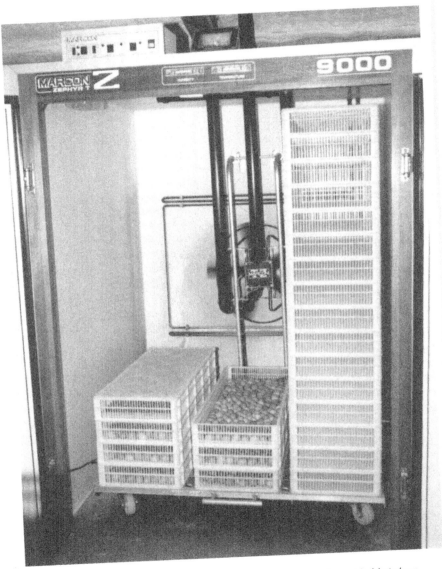

Fig.10.8. Marcon Gamestock Zephyr T 9000 moving–air Hatcher

Opening the ventilators too soon to allow the already hatched chicks to dry off will, of course, lower the humidity and adversely affect the last to hatch. Ventilators should only be opened after all the chicks have hatched, for a chick needs no more oxygen after it has hatched than it did during the process of hatching. Unless the manufacturer's instructions specifically state otherwise, the eggs should be transferred to a pre-warmed hatcher, with the water pots full and the ventilators wide open. The ventilators should be closed right down as soon as about twenty per cent of the eggs show signs of chipping, and not opened again until the entire hatch is off. In commercial hatching, it is the last few percent that decide the profit, not the first few out of the eggs.

If the machine cannot supply this necessary high humidity in the final stages, spraying the eggs with warm water can only have beneficial effects, provided that it is done at the correct time, which is at the end of the dry shell period. To open the incubator in the middle of the hatch to spray with water will kill more chicks than it saves.

Fig. 10.9. Partridge chicks at transfer

189

Drying off

The physical act of hatching requires tremendous effort, and the chick emerges wet and exhausted. It needs at least twelve hours' rest to recover. If moved from the incubator too soon, they can easily get chilled. The modern chick box is so designed that the chicks keep each other warm in an enclosed space, so that on arrival they are 'nest ripe', active, dry, and hungry.

During this period of drying off, the discarded feather sheaths, shells and membranes, together with the first droppings, make a great deal of mess. Bacteria will contaminate some of this. These are bacteria that have entered an egg, but have been held at bay by the natural defences of the developing chick. Once the chick has emerged, these defences are no longer operative, and the spread of bacteria in the warm, moist atmosphere, on an unlimited food supply, is rampant. Just one infected egg can create an enormous build-up of pathogenic bacteria. To put more fresh hatching eggs into this mess is to invite trouble.

HYGIENE

All the incubator debris should be disposed of immediately the chicks have been taken off. Incineration is ideal, but if this is not possible, it should be sealed in a polythene bag before disposal. All the fluff and small pieces of shell should be collected with a vacuum cleaner. Since some spread of fluff is inevitable during this procedure, the whole room should be vacuumed as well, so disposing of any cobwebs and dust which could be future sources of trouble. Because of this disease liability, all commercial establishments use a separate hatching room which is dismantled and sterilized after each hatch.

Everything possible should be removed from the hatcher and washed separately in a detergent disinfectant solution, and the hatcher scrubbed out. Commercial egg sanitants, at about double strength in very hot water, are ideal for this. The hatcher, whilst still wet and warm, should be fumigated. On every available opportunity, the setters should get the same treatment, at least at the beginning and end of every season.

Sterilisation of incubators containing eggs

Where disease is an actual or potential problem, disinfectants should be used within the incubators routinely. Formalin is the most effective, but great care must be taken with its use. Except at the critical times when it should not be used, that is from the twenty-fourth to the ninety-sixth hour after setting and within three days of hatching, it may be used as a weekly routine immediately after setting fresh eggs. The correct concentration for the particular time is vital, as too much exposure will kill the embryo in the shell as well as the germs on it.

Most game farmers use hypochlorite disinfection at the weekly setting of fresh eggs. A fine mist spray, either from an aerosol can or a small hand pump, is directed into the circulating air near the fans. Although this will not sterilize an infected egg shell, it will kill most of the bacteria floating free in the air of the incubator, and so lessen the rate of spread of disease within it.

RECORDING INDIVIDUAL CLUTCHES

All eggs set to hatch should be recorded, for the human memory is a fallible thing. An exercise book, preferably of graph paper, together with a pencil, should be tied to the side of the incubator. This will discourage would-be borrowers of the pencil, and will remind the operator to use it.

The number and species of the eggs, with the date set and the date due, are vital information.

Next should follow the number of eggs weighed and the average weight of one egg. Always work in grammes: 1% of 65 grammes is a much easier sum than 1% of 2¼ ounces.

Using as an example ten pheasant eggs weighing, say, 340 grammes and an incubation period of twenty-four days, a 10% weight loss is 34 grammes, so a simple graph of 40 grammes against twenty-four days will cover all eventualities.

Draw the predicted weight loss on the graph, and mark in the actual weight of the ten eggs at weekly intervals. Humidity control is now an exact science.

Record, too, the number of infertiles thrown out at the first candling, together with any deaths at each weekly session, and finally, the number hatched, and an opinion of the quality of the chicks. An opinion of the estimated correctness of the air cell size, recorded at the time, is invaluable for later comparisons.

Intelligent interpretation of the records, when compared with actual hatching success, will help to pinpoint faults and should increase the next hatches by a significant percentage.

Date set	*June 1ˢᵗ*
Date due to hatch	*June 25ᵗʰ*
Number & species of eggs	*205 Game Pheasants*
Weight of 10 eggs at setting	*340 grams*
Average weight	*34 grams*
1% of average weight	*0.34 grams*
Eggs thrown out	
Infertile	*5*
Deaths by 7ᵗʰ day	*6*
Deaths by 14ᵗʰ day	*2*
Deaths by 21ˢᵗ day	*6*
Dead in shell	*7*
% Infertile	*2.5%*
% Hatch	*87.3%*
Quality chicks	*179*
Remarks, air cell size, etc,	*Eggs bought from game farm*

Fig.10.10. Specimen record

Chapter 11

HATCHING FAILURES

WHY DIDN'T IT HATCH?

Before any answer can be given to this deceptively simple question, the answers to many other questions must be known. The reason could lie in the stock, its nutrition, the egg storage, the incubator room, the incubator or in any aspect of the management of all of them.

In many cases, detailed records will make the answer obvious. All too often the post mortem examination of a single dead in shell chick will produce no obvious cause of death, but quite superficial examination of the incubation records will show a characteristic pattern in the percentages of deaths at the various stages of incubation.

Investigations of hatching problems by the Game Conservancy over many years have shown that 20% of the problems investigated were due to egg storage, 20% were caused by the environment of the incubator, and 20% were due to faulty turning. All the other causes of poor hatches, such as genetic problems, fertility, nutrition, incorrect setting of incubator controls, incorrect humidity, infection, or poor techniques, accounted for less than half the problems investigated.

EXAMINATION OF RECORDS

Percentage hatch and quality of the chicks is the first vital information. Over 86% of good chicks probably can't be improved, and this should be the goal to aim for. Any commercial hatchery that does not consistently attain this figure is losing money. Many aviculturists are satisfied with a hatch of over 70%, but a little attention to detail could improve this. Less than 50% is a waste of eggs and time, and indicates a serious problem.

PERCENTAGE INFERTILE

Up to about 5% infertile eggs can be accepted as inevitable. More than this, points to a problem in the breeding stock or its management. All apparently infertile eggs should be opened and the yolk inspected carefully for any signs of embryonic development. If there are any, the egg was not infertile.

Possible causes of infertility
    Parents too old.
    Parents too young.
    Wrong environment, extremes of temperature, inadequate housing.
    Health, poor incubation, or rearing of parents.
    Poor nutrition or insufficient water.
    Disturbed mating.
    Cross mating.
    No pair bond.
    Non-synchronous breeding condition.
    Preferential mating.
    Too inbred.
    Wrong ratio of cocks to hens.
    Apparent infertility due to poor storage.

EMBRYONIC DEATH

When the remaining eggs are examined after a good hatch and the age at death of each unhatched egg ascertained, it is usual to find that 30% of deaths occurred in the last few days, 30% very early in incubation, and the remaining eggs died randomly throughout the incubation period. After a poor hatch, the distribution of the ages at death can give valuable clues to the cause of death.

Death in the first week
Too many deaths in the first week could be caused by:
    Parental genetics.
    Chilling or overheating of eggs before collection.
    Faulty storage: too warm, too long, or both, with no turning.
    Improper sterilisation.
    Rough handling.
    Faulty incubator temperature, particularly too hot.
    Chilling.
    Inadequate turning.
    Virus infections.
    Vitamin E deficiency.

Unless there has been gross malfunction of the incubator thermostat or the incubator room is wholly unsuitable, death in the first week tends not to be an incubator problem, unless there is a faulty thermometer giving a wildly inaccurate reading.

Death in the second week

Any of the causes of death in the first week can so weaken an embryo at that time that it succumbs later. Some deaths of these weakened embryos will occur during the second week, but the peak of the mortality will not occur till near hatching time.

Heavy mortality in the second week, in the absence of a high mortality in the first week, could be caused by:

Serious vitamin deficiencies in the food.

Galloping infection within the incubator.

Serious mis-settings of incubator controls.

Overheating or chilling, particularly at candling time.

Gross over- or under-humidification.

Inadequate ventilation of incubator.

Death in the third week

For those species of bird with a longer incubation period than twenty-one days, the remainder of the time in the incubator can, as far as causes of death are concerned, be included in the third week. A significant point of interest is that slightly incorrect incubator settings that will hatch an egg with a short incubation period, have more time to affect an egg with a longer incubation period. These eggs do not hatch so well under slightly wrong conditions. This applies particularly to incorrect humidity control and ventilation as well as temperature.

This third and final period is the pay-off time, for mistakes made earlier in incubation are not always apparent until the embryo dies just before it is due to hatch.

Death before the establishment of pulmonary respiration

The change to breathing with its lungs is one of the biggest steps that the embryo makes. Any weakness, either inherent in the egg or caused by adverse conditions imposed upon it, will cause a high mortality at this stage. All too often, at post mortem the chick appears to be perfectly developed; it just died instead of starting to breathe. The beak has not entered the air cell.

All the faults of parent stock management, heredity, egg storage, hygiene, and disease make their mark now.

In the absence of a previously raised death rate, death at this stage, combined with a high death rate of chicks that had started to breathe, indicates an incubator problem. High death rates in both the first and third weeks indicate either a genetic or egg storage problem.

The usual incubator causes of death at this stage are:

Temperature too high.

Temperature too low.

Widely fluctuating temperature.

Bringing the eggs up from storage to incubation temperature too quickly.

Insufficient humidity.

Too much humidity.

Poor ventilation.

Inadequate turning.

It is important to remember that mistakes made earlier in incubation, such as temporary over-heating, chilling, and failure to turn in the early days, although not appearing to kill the egg at that stage, have so weakened it that it dies now.

Poor egg storage, widely fluctuating temperature due to an unsuitable incubator room, and failure to turn sufficiently are the most commonly encountered causes of death before the change to lung breathing. Where death is due to infection, the pattern is usually that of increasing numbers of deaths at all stages of incubation, with a large peak just before hatching time.

Death after breathing is established

These are usually referred to as dead in shell. The chick may or may not have chipped the shell. All the causes of a weakened embryo, either inherent in the egg or produced by poor incubation techniques, will cause death at this stage as well as before breathing commenced. The chick is just too weak to hatch. Chilling and excessive jolting on transfer to the hatcher will also kill a percentage of otherwise good chicks. Incorrect conditions within the hatcher will prevent successful emergence of a previously healthy chick.

Fig. 11.1. Deaths while in shell (see over page)

Early death
  A   Shows typical blood rings of death in the first few days
  B   Shows death in the seventh day. The vascular pattern has disintegrated, and the embryo is an amorphous blob
Mid-period death
  C   Died on the tenth day. Note the position of the ring of blood around
       the edge of the membranes, and the total absence of recognisable blood vessels
  D   This is a double-yolked mandarin egg, with two embryos. Both have died but both amniotic sacs are intact and can be clearly seen.
Late death
  E   Has virtually decomposed, and should have been thrown out at a previous candling. Note the large air cell and the total disintegration
  F   Has been dead a few days. Note the fuzzy edge between the air cell and egg contents, the complete absence of blood vessels and the clear space at the small end — unabsorbed albumen
  G   Further example of late death
  H   Death after the embryo has entered the air space. The demarcation line is no longer sharp and there was, of course, no movement. The lip of the beak can just be seen protruding into the air space

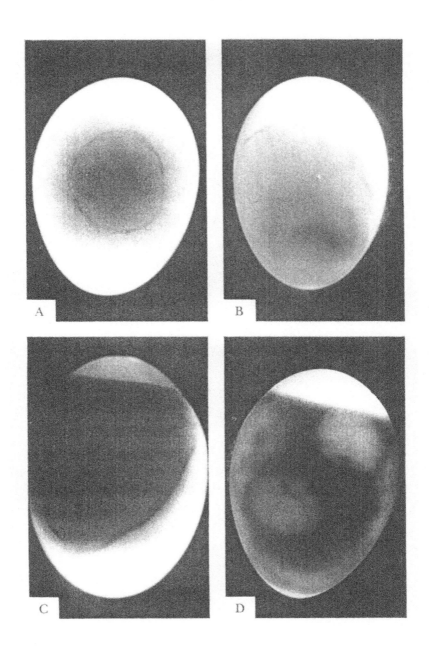

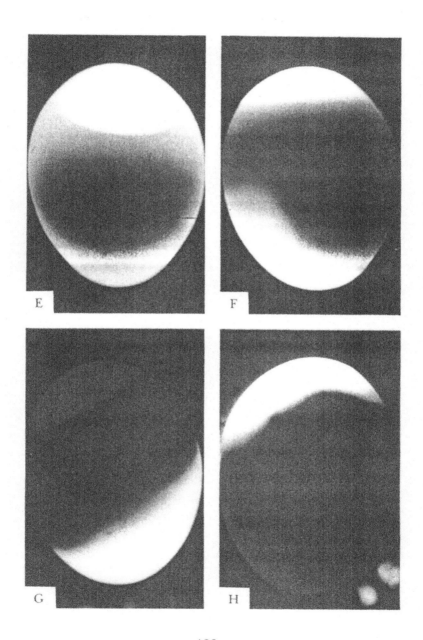

Examination of dead in shell

It is sometimes possible to ascertain the cause of death by examination of the unhatched eggs, in conjunction with examination of the chicks that did hatch. The two together often produce a diagnostic picture.

The technique of examining an unhatched egg is very simple and requires no special knowledge. First note whether or not the egg had pipped, or the chick in chipping had started to rotate round the egg.

Insufficient moisture in the hatcher, particularly with pheasants and turkeys, is a common cause of large and unnecessary losses. Under these circumstances, many of the eggs have chips most of the way round them, but the tough dry membranes have not split, so that the chick is imprisoned within its egg, unable to escape. It died of exhaustion.

Where there has been too much moisture in the early stages, the chick is large and soft, and the albumen has not all been absorbed. The chick has pierced the shell and its beak protrudes through the hole. It is unable to withdraw it to make another chip, because the unused albumen leaks out through the hole and, having a consistency of the old fashioned wood glues, sets hard round it. This glued beak in the hole is very common in ducks that have had too much moisture in the earlier part of incubation.

This picture can also be produced by wrong temperatures all the way through, particularly fluctuating temperatures, but is exaggerated by insufficient humidity at hatching time.

Having ascertained whether or not the egg had chipped and if there was anything characteristic about it. Next remove the top of the egg, either with a pair of scissors or with a knife, and look at the air cell, noting the size and whether the beak is in the air cell, or if the chick is malpositioned.

Remove the chick and look for excess albumen, which will be present in many if they have been over-humidified or, sometimes, if the average temperature has been too low. Infected eggs often have a foul odour with discoloured fluid around the embryo. In many cases of infection, however, the chick appears perfectly normal, but culture of the yolk sac, liver, and lungs will give large numbers of bacteria.

Where the average temperature has been too high all the way through, the chicks tend to be small; they have beaks in the air cell but a knob of yolk sac unabsorbed. Such dead in shell chicks are often sticky to the touch. Too little humidity can also produce sticky little chicks glued into their shells. If the humidity at hatching is high enough to prevent any further evaporation of this glue, making it even stickier, many of the chicks will manage to hatch, but will be small, not very active, and often have a higher than normal death rate in the early weeks.

Examination of the chicks that hatch
First ascertain the percentage hatch of fertile eggs. Anything under an 86% hatch could be improved. It is more convenient to consider the whole picture produced by incubator faults than to try to give the causes of any particular abnormality.

Incubator too hot. The first chicks out tend to be early; in extreme cases, up to forty-eight hours before the expected date of hatch. Many of these early chicks will be small and weak, with unhealed navels or even a knob of yolk sac protruding. The remainder of the hatch drags on, with many weak chicks struggling to be late hatchers. Minor malformations, such as crooked toes, are common. There is also a high proportion of late dead in shell.

Incubator too cool. The first signs of hatching tend to be late, usually by at least a day. Perfectly normal chicks are still hatching up to two days late. The total hatch is often reasonable, but the chicks are large and soft, and a bit sluggish in getting going. A few will have malformations such as crooked toes and wry neck. There will be some dead in shell, but not as many as are produced by too high a temperature. Many of the late hatchers tend to be a bit sticky.

Too little moisture in the setting period. The chicks are always small and weak, with a very high proportion of dead in shell. The air cells of such dead eggs are always much too large.

Too much moisture in the setting period. The chicks are large and blobby, often coated with sticky albumen. There is also a high percentage of unhatched pipped eggs, often with a live embryo imprisoned inside.

Too little moisture in the hatcher. The hatch starts well, the early hatchers getting out quickly, but those that follow are in difficulties. Many that do get out have pieces of shell sticking to them, but many fail to get out, being strapped in their shells by tough membranes. If the setting conditions have been sufficiently near the optimum to produce a live chick but not an active hatcher, the inner egg membranes dry out, preventing the chick from rotating by causing it to adhere to the shell. Opening the hatcher door, just to see how they are getting on, produces such a picture.

Too much moisture in the hatcher. It is virtually impossible to get too much humidity in the hatcher, provided that there is adequate ventilation. Where there is no ventilation and a very high humidity, the chicks are soft and mushy and appear to be gasping for breath. This is not caused by the high humidity but by the lack of fresh air.

Setting stale eggs. Eggs that have been stored tend to produce smaller chicks that take longer to hatch. Collecting eggs over a three-week period will give a high apparent infertility and early death rate, with many dead in shell, and a prolonged 'draggy' hatch.

TROUBLE SHOOTING CHART

Symptoms of Trouble			Probable Causes
1	**Eggs Clear**	(a)	Improper mating.
	No blood ring or	(b)	Males undernourished.
	embryo growth	(c)	Eggs too old.
		(d)	Male sterility or preferential mating.
2	**Clear with Blood Ring**	(a)	Incubator temperature too high.
	or partial		
	Development	(b)	Eggs chilled.
		(c)	Eggs too old.
3	**Dead Germs**	(a)	Wrong incubator temperature.
	Embryos dying 12/18		
	days and chicks	(b)	Lack of ventilation.
	fully formed, dying	(c)	Incorrect turning.
	without pipping	(d)	Heredity.
4	**Dead in Shell**	(a)	As in 3(a).
		(b)	As in 3(c).
		(c)	Low average humidity.
		(d)	Too high average humidity especially with DUCKS.
		(e)	Infectious disease.
5	**Abnormal Chicks**	(a)	Too low average humidity.
	Shell sticking		
		(b)	Low humidity at hatching time.
		(c)	Incorrect turning.
	Sticky chicks	(a)	Low temperature
		(b)	Too much humidity

203

Rough navels	(a)	High incubator temperature
Small chicks	(a)	Small eggs
	(b)	Low humidity
	(c)	High incubator temperature
Large soft-bodied chicks	(a)	Low average temperature
	(b)	Too high humidity
	(c)	Bad room ventilation
Short down	(a)	High temperature
	(b)	Low humidity
Heavy breathing	(a)	Too high humidity
Turkey help-outs	(a)	Low humidity at hatching time
	(b)	Temperature too high in hatching tray

6 **Malformed chicks**

Crossed beak	(a)	Heredity
Crooked toes	(a)	Too high temperature
	(b)	Too low temperature
Splayed legs	(a)	Too high temperature
	(b)	Hatching tray too smooth
Bent neck	(a)	Too long hatching due to low temperature
	(b)	Too long hatching due to low humidity

7 **Draggy Hatch**
Some chicks early
but slow finishing

	(a)	Temperature too high
	(b)	Wide difference in age of eggs
	(c)	Membranes too dry at pipping time

8	**Delayed hatch** Eggs late pipping and slow finishing	(a)	Average temperature too low
9	**Bad eggs**	(a)	Excessive humidity
		(b)	Hair cracks when setting

Chapter 12

BROODING AND REARING

Once hatched, the chicks of all species of bird are unable to maintain their body temperature unaided. They need frequent pauses in their search for food when they can rest and warm up. Those that hatch blind, naked and helpless need more or less continual brooding to keep them warm and feeding very frequently. Although the eggs of these birds can be hatched in incubators, artificial rearing is a very time-consuming business and does not often succeed. Those chicks that hatch downed and active arc much easier to rear artificially. Pheasants, partridges and quail need a lot of brooding, as do most of the smaller ducks; but diving ducks, geese and swans do not need as much. Nutrition is also very important.

REARING BY BROODY HEN
If the hen has hatched the chicks herself, she should be allowed to brood them for about twelve hours until they are nest ripe and active. If they have been incubator hatched, they should be introduced to her gently in the sitting box, and she should be allowed to brood them for several hours before being moved to a coop and run. Most broodies that have been sitting for a while can be persuaded to take to day old chicks if they are introduced underneath her a few at a time in the box she has been sitting in, and preferably in subdued light.

Once she has accepted them and the chicks have snuggled underneath her for warmth and safety, they can be moved to a prepared coop and run. The coop and the ground underneath it must be dry. A handful of wood shavings, peat, or sand on mown grass is ideal. The hen should be confined to the coop with the food and water pot just outside where she can reach it, but not scratch it all over the place. The run must be small, so that the chicks cannot escape and get chilled. Short grass is ideal for the run, but if this is not available, sand or small gravel will do. In either case, the coop and run must be moved to a clean ground every day.

ARTIFICIAL BROODING

The requirements of the chicks are the same, whether they are reared by their parents, a broody hen, or under artificial heat. In artificial brooding, a heater supplies the heat and the food and water made freely available. The heat can be supplied by electricity; gas, oil, or paraffin, and appliances are commercially made to care for anything from single chicks to hundreds of thousands. It has been proved many times over that all species of chick thrive better if they can choose their own temperature, i.e. if they have a warm area to which they can return and rest and a colder area where they can run around and feed. As they grow and feather, the temperature in the warm area can be reduced, usually by raising the heat source a short distance each day. It is vitally important that a chick never gets chilled. Although the chick appears to recover on warming, a very high proportion of such chilled chicks develops gastro-intestinal problems or failure of the liver and kidneys and succumbs several days later. A chick that is too hot gets very distressed and soon dies.

THE DOMESTIC CHICKEN

Many, many appliances have been marketed in the past for this, but most have been superseded by the infra-red electric heater. This is suspended over the floor so that the temperature directly underneath is at incubating temperature, i.e. about 99°F (37.2°C). Right in the very center it will be too hot for the chicks, but a temperature gradient will be created from just too hot at the center down to room temperature away from the heat. Each chick can choose its own position. A ring of corrugated cardboard around the heated area prevents the chicks from straying too far from the heat. Food and water pots are placed around the heated area, but not in it, so that the birds do not have to look far for food. A 150 watt heater will accommodate two dozen or more chicks. Large broiler sheds holding several hundred thousand day-old chicks use gas heaters on the same principle, several thousand chicks being confined under each heater, but it has been found that the birds do better in lots of about five hundred under each heater.

After about forty-eight hours the ring of cardboard is enlarged to allow them more space, and after a few days it is removed altogether. For the first week the lamp is raised a few inches to reduce the temperature of the hot center by a few degrees and is raised further, at weekly intervals until it is down to about 60°F (15.5C) at around six weeks, by which time they should be fully feathered and independent of the extra heating.

Fig. 12.1. A. B. Keepwarm electric hen (brooder)

The birds are the best guide to the correct temperature. If they are huddled under the center of the heater, they are too cold. There should be a center spot, which is too hot with a ring of comfortable chicks around it. If the empty center is too large, the birds are too hot and the lamp can be raised.

GAME PHEASANTS AND PARTRIDGES

These can be reared in exactly the same manner as chickens, as they have the same heat requirements. They do, however, need a very high quality protein food. The chicks are much more active and positively suicidal. If there is a hole they can get out of to get chilled, they will find it. They also manage to drown themselves in the water pots if these are not obstructed with stones, and get stuck between food and water containers if these are too close together or too close to the cardboard.

Fig. 12.2. A.B. Isothermic moving-air brooder for Parrots and similar species

Their biggest vice is feather picking, which leads to cannibalism. Pheasants under a white light start eating each other by the second day of life. Using a red light can reduce this. Where large numbers are reared together intensively they need to be in semi-darkness; even then they will probably need to be de-beaked or fitted with plastic bits to stop it.

Most small batches of game pheasants are reared under an electric hen. This is a flat heater with short legs, rather like a table. A short piece of cloth hangs down round the edges, underneath which the birds brood in total darkness, coming out into the light to feed.

They are usually housed in small wooden or metal huts, and the birds have access to an outside run almost from the first day. The size of the run is increased as the birds grow, until they are released on the site where they have been reared.

Most of the ornamental pheasants tend to be hatch in very small clutches, and are even worse feather pickers than their game cousins, when confined in small breeding boxes.

A small brooder box can easily be constructed. It needs a floor area of about 18 inches by 12 inches, sides about 12 inches high, with an electric light bulb suspended about 6 inches from the floor at one end.

If the light is too bright and causes feather picking, it can be placed in a clay flowerpot, which will retain the heat, or be replaced with a ceramic low wattage heater. A floor of small mesh wire netting saves the daily chore of cleaning out the droppings. Most pheasants can fly after a few days, so it also needs a wire netting cover to prevent them jumping out.

Fig. 12.3. Marcon Gamestock 100 B electric hen (brooder)

QUAIL

Quail are produced commercially by being brooded on the floor on sand, peat, or woodshavings, in exactly the same manner as pheasants, but because they are so small they can easily get out and get lost. They rear very well in small brooding boxes. Their heat requirements are the same as chickens.

DUCKS

Ducks not only require a great deal of water to drink, they also splash it everywhere and make very messy liquid droppings. They can be reared just like chickens but will need cleaning out every day.

Commercial ducks are reared very successfully on wire mesh or expanded metal floors. It is becoming fashionable to rear the ornamental species in brooder boxes which have wire floors except for a small piece of carpet or similar material under the light; which is washed every day. The easiest way to rear ornamental ducks is under an infra-red heater bulb on a floor of wood shavings. For the first two days the ducklings are confined near the heat by a ring of cardboard, and are given water to drink from small automatic chick bowls. As soon as they are all feeding well, the cardboard is removed, giving them access to a small plastic pond. This pond is raised up from the floor on a wire mesh grille, and the ducks have to run up a concrete ramp to get to it. They can swim and splash as much as they like, and the surplus runs through the grille and down a drain. The food is still kept by the heaters so the ducks have to run between the two. Most of the water on their feet comes off on the ramp so that the litter remains dry.

Most of the dropping are deposited either in or near the water. The level of the water in the small pond must, of course, be maintained automatically by a ball valve; it only needs emptying once per day. Under this system, as many as forty ornamentals can be reared together, and batches of a hundred mallard type with very little cleaning out, except at the end. After the first week, the light is raised a few inches. By the third week, the ducks are off heat and ready to go to outside runs.

Mandarins, Carolinas, and the Goldeneye have small claws on the feet to enable them to climb vertical surfaces. These species must be confined to very smooth cardboard or they will climb out and get chilled.

Domestic ducks and those of the mallard family are born looking for food and start eating instantly, as, incidentally, do most of the pheasant family. If a little freshly chopped grass is sprinkled on the food, they will soon start investigating it, and eating. Live food is, in the main, unnecessary.

Most of the ornamental ducks, Carolina and Goldeneye in particular, can starve to death while sitting on a pile of the most nutritious food that the poultry industry can devise, not knowing that it is food. They must be taught to eat. The easiest way to teach them is to put one or two teachers in with them. The smallest duck of the previous hatch is ideal if he is not more than two days older. Equally good are one or two Mallard ducklings, hatched simultaneously just for this very purpose. The natural food of most ducklings is small live food, such as insects, moving on the surface of the water. If some chick and small pieces of freshly chopped grass are put into a shallow tin, with water allowed to drip into it from above, the duckings will go for the moving grass and start eating it.

Most ducklings cannot resist investigating pretty-coloured objects. "Smarties", sugarcoated chocolate beans, placed on the dry food dish get full attention and become very sticky. They are too big to be swallowed, but get coated with sticky crumbs and shoot all over the place. The crumbs stick to the beak and get eaten.

All species of ducks should be started on very high quality chick crumbs, but after a week or so should move on to growers rations, or problems can arise with slipped wings and hock tendons.

GEESE

Geese can be reared in exactly the same manner as ducks, and can, in fact, be reared with them. They do, however, need as much green food as they can eat from the very start; to dilute the too-concentrated chick crumbs. They should be off heat by two weeks old. Goslings must have something to imprint on or they become miserable and don't eat and grow. Batches of eight or more imprint on each other, but if there are only one or two, they are far better off with some ducks for the first few days than on their own.

The odd early clutch of only one or two are probably better off if reared by a broody hen.

TURKEYS AND GUINEAFOWL

These can be reared with the same methods as used for chickens, and do very well under these systems. They need good quality chick crumbs, of high protein, with anti-coccidiostat and anti-blackhead drugs added to the feed. The heat requirements are very similar to those of chickens.

Fig. 12.4. Measuring the development of a Houbara Bustard chick

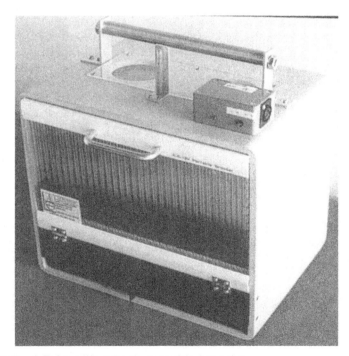

Fig. 12.5. A.B.Newlife 12v dc portable brooder

Chapter 13

INCUBATION TECHNIQUES IN THE NEW MILLENNIUM

THE YEARS 1979-2002

After 23 years, the original content of this book is still regarded as the bible of incubation but in the intervening years a little has been learned about the ways in which successful hatches with difficult and endangered species can be achieved. Improved knowledge about the requirements of certain eggs, the availability of more advanced equipment and the commitment of private breeders have all contributed to these successes. Today we hear of equipment being adapted for species as varied as Honey-eaters to Ostriches with very successful results.

Equipment

The latest types of incubators are highly accurate in temperature control using the latest solid-state electronic technology. Manufacturers now take great care to see that the airflow over and around the eggs is even, preventing high and low temperature spots. For those embarking on incubating eggs from species such as Parrots, Birds of Prey, and other exotic birds, the moving air type incubator is now preferable to a still air machine, as it ensures an even flow of air around the eggs. New ideas are being introduced to ensure that successful hatches are obtained using the simplest methods of operation for the operator.

Turning

Another aspect of the latest incubators is automatic egg turning. The smaller and less expensive models have their turning controlled by a fixed speed motor/gearbox combination, which provides the motion to the turning mechanism, allowing eggs to turn through 90° and back every 2 hours. The more expensive models incorporate time-clocks which can be programmed to turn eggs through the same angles every 10 minutes in a 24 hour period, if required. As already mentioned, there are three methods of turning:

1) Rolling eggs from side to side

2) Rotating the eggs over from side to side through the vertical position with the pointed end down

3) The eggs held pointed end downwards in plastic egg trays which move through 90^0.

The eggs of some difficult species need to be turned on their sides for the first 10-15 days, then vertically until internal pip. One manufacturer has produced a small incubator that facilitates both methods concurrently, ensuring continuity of the eggs' environment so that transfer to another incubator is unnecessary. With the demand for so many sizes of eggs requiring incubation, another problem arises, in that an egg on rollers has to be turned through 180° and back. In the past this has been achieved by selecting the correct size of roller for the species concerned.

In 2000, A.B. Incubators introduced their Newlife Mk6 Incubator, where the roller rotation can be controlled to suit the requirement of an egg from certain species. Also, rubber rings of various sizes were fitted to the rollers to accommodate large eggs with pointed ends holding them in position so that they were level and rotated in their own plane, thus preventing them barrelling up to one end of the rollers.

Humidity

A few years ago the humidity requirement when incubating difficult eggs was not fully understood and a tray of water on the floor of the machine was thought to be adequate. Today, with better knowledge and understanding of the egg humidity requirement for individual species, an incubator needs to be able to provide variable levels of humidity.

A feature of the original Anderson Brown designed machine was consistently controlled humidity at a set level using a wet bulb system. A sensor placed alongside the thermometer in the wet bulb wick monitors the rise and fall of the temperature in the machine. Once the depression falls below the electronic control setting, a solenoid valve opens to allow more water in. When the set humidity level is achieved through vapourisation, the valve closes. Further air changes will stimulate the sensor to repeat the process.

Some manufacturers are using the latest solid state sensing devices, which measure humidity by sensing the moisture in the air across a bi-metallic strip in the sensor. This eliminates the need for a wet bulb system and for the regular replacement of wicks to maintain an accurate reading. The main disadvantage, however, is that the bi-metallic strips tend to become contaminated with dust or fluff after a hatch. This can cause an inaccurate reading, and can stop the supply of water for humidity. These devices are not easily cleaned or recalibrated to their original working level, therefore such devices are not recommended until they have been perfected to cope with such conditions. The latest models have sensors, which have some protection against dust etc., and can work in harsh conditions. This has come about through research into the requirements for humidity monitoring in computer rooms and laboratories.

A.B. Incubators have introduced their new humidity controller as a stand-alone unit, which is designed for use in machines without humidity control fitted as standard. The main advantage is that it is microprocessor controlled using a sensor which, in turn, controls a peristaltic pump putting the required amount of water into the incubator to a pre-programmed level of relative humidity.

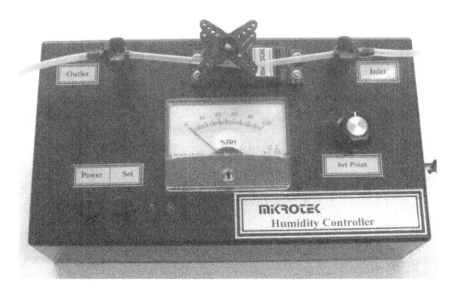

Fig. 13.1. A.B. Mikrotek Humidity Controller

Monitoring conditions

The mercury thermometer has traditionally been the best and most accurate instrument to measure temperature, but with the advent of small electronic circuits, the digital thermometer is increasingly being used. Readings can be seen clearly, and the repeatable accuracy is coming within acceptable limits, around 0.1°C. Digital thermometers can now be obtained at a sensible price.

Digital meters for humidity are also becoming available. These measure the humidity and display it as % RH. At present, the accuracy is between +/- 5% for meters at a sensible price. However, in time, as sensors become more accurate and more available at a lower price, due to mass production, the meter price is certain to come down.

Moving air hatchers

For many years, the traditional method of hatching eggs has been to use a still air incubator and most gamekeepers would not consider moving to anything else. The advent of large hatcheries perfecting the moving air incubator has raised interest in moving towards this method. Although the still air hatcher was successful, there were some disadvantages. The number of eggs per compartment was limited and, should the door of the hatcher be opened during the hatch period, the humidity would take some hours to recover. This results in a delay in hatching. On the other hand, the moving air hatcher will recover its humidity in only a few minutes, as a paddle or fan is used to circulate the air evenly. The quantity of eggs able to be hatched in one area can be the same as those placed in the original setter.

Certainly, from tests carried out using small, moving air hatchers, the quality of the chicks hatched is improved. The chicks retain their strength, being able to leave the shell quickly with minimal energy expenditure.

Future methods of control

The advancement of miniature components in solid-state electrical devices has already enabled microprocessor controls to be fitted to large commercial setters. Temperature and humidity requirements are entered and stored in a memory base. It is anticipated that smaller models will be similarly equipped in the near future. Such systems have other advantages. The actual temperature is checked against that set and, should the actual temperature exceed the setting by one degree up or down for any reason, an alarm is triggered. A similar miniature controller will also be available for the control of humidity within the cabinet. Breeders of difficult species are now realizing the great advantages if they invest in these accurate controls, and they are pressing manufacturers for such systems to be fitted to standard equipment. The extra costs can easily be recouped by the hatching of just a few extra eggs each season.

A.B. Incubators introduced the first small machine to use a microprocessor temperature control two years ago. Its main advantage has been to give stability to the temperature where there is a mains voltage fluctuation into the incubation room. It can also operate with accuracy against a fixed point temperature programme. This was the forerunner to the humidity control mentioned above.

Techniques to improve hatchability

The chicken and turkey industries have been using weight loss as a method of monitoring the progress of an egg through incubation and, as already mentioned, most eggs lose between 12-15% of their original weight through moisture loss. If that loss can be kept to within the requirements of the individual species by increasing or decreasing the humidity in the cabinet, the likelihood of a successful hatch increases dramatically. In the early 80's Cornell University in the United States pioneered the use of weight loss to increase the hatch rate of the Peregrine Falcon. This method of incubation has now progressed to many other species such as Parrots, Pheasants, Penguins and Ratites with excellent results.

Weight loss techniques

When using weight loss as a way of improving hatchability there are certain guidelines to consider.

a) The egg must have been freshly laid. The time for the loss to be monitored is from the setting of the egg until the internal pip, when the chick breaks into the air space and starts to breathe.

b) To calculate the weight loss:
   (i)   The egg is weighed on a set of scales which are accurate to 100th of a gram (0.0l g),
   (ii)   Calculate what 15% of the total is,
   (iii)   Divide the result of (ii) by the number of days from setting to internal pip. This will give you the ideal loss per day throughout the incubation period,
   (iv)   Draw a graph as shown in Fig. 10.10 with the weight up the left side and the number of days across the bottom. The weight loss expected each day until internal pip is plotted for reference.

It is wrong to think that all eggs will lose the same amount of moisture during incubation. This may be possible in the wild but is not so in captivity, due to many factors. To monitor a clutch of valuable eggs, each one needs to be individually weighed daily and to have its own plot on the graph. The amount of weight lost from an egg can be controlled by either increasing or decreasing the humidity in the incubator. An egg losing too much moisture needs increased humidity, whereas an egg not losing very much needs a drier machine.

When dealing with large numbers of eggs being incubated at the same time, such as game pheasants, weighing a small number from the batch can give some indication as to how the eggs are progressing and will allow compensatory humidity adjustments to be made. When dealing with small numbers of eggs on a regular basis, most breeders invest in additional small incubators that are run at different humidity levels. The eggs are transferred between incubators according to their graph readings.

Density loss techniques

This is a further technique that is used to calculate the moisture loss of an egg to a much finer degree. Some people find it difficult to understand what density is. If a fresh egg is placed in a bucket of water, the egg will sink and therefore the density is greater than 1. On the other hand, if the same egg is placed in a bucket of water near the end of its incubation period, it will float, giving it a density of less than 1. At some point, if a similar procedure is carried out during incubation, the egg will neither float nor sink, but be held in suspension.

To use the density loss formula, the egg has to be weighed and then divided by its volume. As most of us learnt at school, to find the volume of a regular rectangular object, you multiply the length by the height by the breadth. Since the height and the breadth of an egg are usually the same, there is a simple mathematical way of working out the volume, by measuring the egg's length with a micrometer and then multiplying the length by its breadth twice and finally multiplying by an accepted correction factor.

Length x breadth x breadth x 0.51 = volume of the egg
(L x B x B x 0.51= volume).

The correction factor has been calculated to take account of the egg's elliptical shape and is used to compensate for the egg being oval and not a rectangle. In the case above, the correction factor = 0.51. This factor changes slightly between eggs of different species but usually this does not exceed 0.04 at the most, which will make little difference to the density graph.

Example: An egg from a pair of Roulroul Partridge

Three measurements are required.
Weight in grams = 20.2g
Length in centimeters = 3.619
Breadth in centimeters = 3.234
Volume = 3.619 x 3.234 x 3.234 x 0.51 = 19.304 cc.

Dividing the weight by the above volume gives the density of 1.046.

The calculation to find the volume is usually done when the egg is fresh. It is then weighed every one or two days and the result divided by the volume (weight + volume). The figure of interest is the average daily density loss. In the Roulroul Partridge example, the daily density loss is 0.010. This figure varies between different species. If the density is too high, and the egg is placed in a high humidity incubator, the density loss will slow down. Conversely, if the egg is placed in too dry an incubator, the loss will increase. This is the same concept as used in weight loss measurement, but has distinct advantages. As eggs vary in size within a clutch, it is not possible to give an average daily weight loss figure. A large egg will lose more weight per day than a smaller egg from the same species. However, an average daily density loss can be obtained because size and shape are taken into account.

Once the technique is mastered, the use of weight loss graphs is not necessary, but can be very informative. The graphs shown in Figs. 13.3 and 13.3 show ten Roulroul Partridge eggs. One graph shows the weight loss and the other, the density loss. These graphs show the two advantages of density loss techniques. Firstly, it is noticeable that the lines are drawn very close together on the density graph compared with the weight loss graph. Imagine that a Roulroul Partridge egg is found which has been partially incubated for an unknown period. To discover how long it has been incubated, it is weighed and found to be 20 grams. By looking at a weight loss graph, it would not be possible to determine whether the egg has just been laid or is just ready to hatch. By working out the egg density, in this example 0.90, it is possible to establish that the egg is between 12 and 14 days in development. In those species where the eggs are impossible to candle, the density loss technique is a very useful tool. It is noticeable when working out a density loss graph that nearly all the eggs start at between 1.03 and 1.05. The most dense part of an egg is the shell itself. An egg with a high start density, say in the case of Roulroul partridge, with a density of 1.08, gives a good idea that the shell is thick. This egg will need to be placed in an incubator with a lower humidity than normal. The opposite applies when an egg has a low start density. Then it can be assumed it has a thin shell and will need a higher humidity in the incubator to stop it from losing too much weight/density.

Monitoring equipment

In large hatcheries all the temperature and humidity levels in each setter and hatcher are automatically recorded on a database for future reference in case of problems during incubation. In addition, each setter has its own pre-programmed computer control, to meet the temperature and humidity needs of individual species' eggs. We are now beginning to see similar systems being installed in several zoo and wildlife breeding stations where close control of a number of

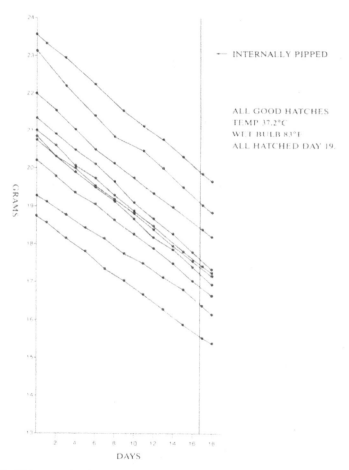

Fig.13.2. This graph shows the weight loss of 10 Roulroul partridge eggs against the days of incubation

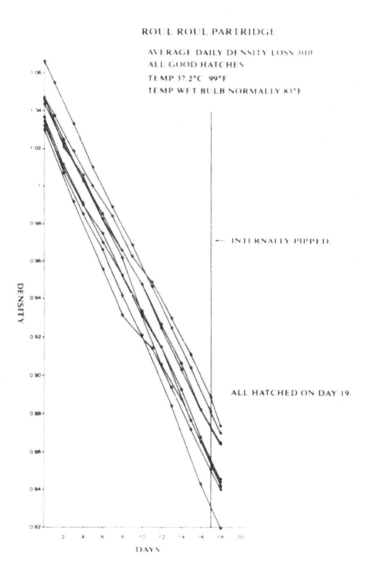

ROUL ROUL PARTRIDGE

AVERAGE DAILY DENSITY LOSS .010
ALL GOOD HATCHES
TEMP 37.2°C 99°F
TEMP WET BULB NORMALLY 83°F

— INTERNALLY PIPPED.

ALL HATCHED ON DAY 19.

Fig.13.3. This graph shows the density lost from 10 Roulroul
partridge eggs against the days of incubation

machines is needed. Each machine has a sensor wired to a central control so that the operator can immediately see if there is a problem in any particular machine, or a print out can be obtained of the performance that has taken place. Warning systems which alert the operator about incorrect temperature levels, or an electrical supply failure are also incorporated.

Portable low voltage incubators and brooders
The increased interest in breeding rare and endangered species has created a need for portable incubators for transporting eggs (from breeders to people who are prepared to incubate and hand rear the resultant chicks). Low voltage brooders are then used to bring the resultant chicks home particularly with parrot species and, to a lesser extent with touracos. These units are usually powered from the cigarette lighter socket of the vehicular transport, or in some cases via a car battery. The machine is very basic having only temperature control with a failsafe warning device, but with no control over turning or humidity. The design pays most attention to retaining heat and keeping the current consumption from the battery to the minimum. There is no ventilation included as the eggs are only subjected to a portable incubator for a limited time, which will not affect their progress. For longer periods the lid is lifted to replenish air for a few seconds every 4-6 hours. Some portable incubators have multiple controls, allowing various input voltages, so that the units can function on different mains supplies around the world. Some have cooler units fitted so that eggs due to hatch can be kept at the required temperature even when the ambient heat in which the incubator is required to work is higher than the operating temperature.

Portable incubators have been in limited use for many years, in particular for collecting wildfowl eggs from Iceland and Alaska. Clearance should be obtained from an airline before transporting such equipment in functional mode as the aircraft's navigational instruments may be affected by the electronic components. Portable brooders pose an even greater problem than portable incubators with regard to heat retention, as there has to be ventilation for the chicks. A balance is achieved between air intake and current consumption so that there is not too great a drain on the battery supply. Most units are designed to work from 12 volts DC supply.

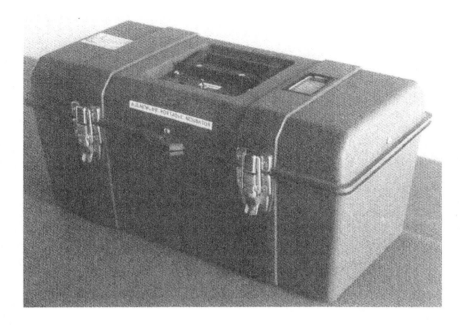

Fig.13.4. A.B. 12v dc Portable Incubator

RATITES

With the increasing interest in ostrich farming, the major incubator companies are producing machines to cater for larger quantities of eggs, e.g. 500-1000 eggs. The manufacturer's instructions should always be adhered to for success when dealing with large numbers of eggs. However, for those who wish to incubate only a few eggs, the following can be used as a general guide to incubation, hatching and rearing ratites, but it must be borne in mind that shells from this order of birds vary in porosity within clutches.

Storage of eggs

Normally eggs being laid at around one per day need to be collected over a period of seven days or so, to give a large enough batch to incubate and hatch together. Therefore the method of storage is important. The eggs should be placed on their sides in a box containing dry sand, in an area where the temperature is no more than 15°C (60°F) with an average humidity around 55%RH. Higher temperature and humidity can cause damage to the embryos; similarly, lower temperature and humidity can also cause problems. For future information, the eggs should be marked with the reference number of the hen laying the egg and with the date laid, and the eggs should be turned over twice a day during storage.

OSTRICH

Average egg size   length   150 - 158mm
                                                       width   125 - 130mm
(size varies according to sub-species and age of hen)
                                                       weight   1207 - 1525g
Artificial incubation   42 - 45 days

Incubation   temperature (moving air)   35.6°-36.0°C
                    humidity   24°C wet bulb reading = 41% RH
Incubation   temperature (still-air machines)
                    for only a single layer of eggs   36°C @ 30% RH

(For areas with high ambient humidity, run the incubator dry.)

Egg weight loss should be 15% before internal pip for most eggs. For large numbers of eggs, select 10 eggs to obtain an average weight loss.

Turning
    The eggs are placed on their sides and turned 3 - 7 times a day by hand. With automatic turning machines the eggs are placed on their sides secured in a basket or holder and turned every hour through 90°. It is also an advantage to turn end over end in addition prior to internal pip should the eggs be incubated on their sides. However where large numbers are concerned, commercial hatcheries have setters where the eggs are held vertically in trays. The trays are turned through 90° once an hour.
Hatching
    At internal pip, place the eggs in a hatcher on their sides. No turning is required. In larger machines a single stage process can be employed. All the eggs are placed in the setter at one time and hatched together in specially designed containers. The humidity in the setter is increased at the time of internal pip.
Brooding
    As soon as the chicks are dry, place in a brooder box heated to 32.2°C (90°F). Without a parent to control this movements the chicks will tend to stray, so the brooding area should not be too large and the floor covering being made of a non-slip material.

RHEA

Average egg size	length	117 - 136mm
	width	80 - 93mm
	weight	424 - 638g

Artificial incubation   35 - 40 days
Incubation   temperature (moving air)   36.0°C
                  humidity   27°C wet bulb reading = 45% RH
Egg weight loss should be 15% before internal pip for most eggs. For large numbers,
10 eggs should be selected to obtain an average weight loss.
Turning   treated the same as Ostrich
Hatching   as Ostrich
Hatching temperature   set @ 1°C lower than the incubation temperature   35.0°C
Humidity   32.0°C wet bulb reading = 80% RH
Brooding   Once hatched the chicks are moved to a brooder box heated
                       to 32.2°C (90°F) to dry off, then as with Ostrich into an
                       enclosure to prevent them straying

EMU

Average egg size	length	135mm
	width	92mm
	weight	662 - 756g

Artificial incubation perieod   49 - 52days
Incubation   temperature (moving air)   37.0°C
                  humidity   23.0°C wet bulb reading = 30%RH
Egg weight loss should be 15% before internal pip for most eggs. For larger numbers,
10 eggs should be selected to obtain the average weight loss.
Turning   treated the same as Ostrich
Hatching   as Ostrich
Hatching temperature   set @ 1°C lower than the incubation temperature   36.0°C
Humidity   33.0°C wet bulb reading = 80%RH
Brooding   treated as Ostrich

CASSOWARY

Average egg size	length	120mm - 150mm
	width	85 - 98mm
	weight	373 - 664g

Artificial incubation period   52 - 63 days
Incubation   temperature (moving air)   36.0°C
                  humidity   30.5°C wet bulb reading = 67% RH
Egg weight loss should be 15% before internal pip. Eggs are very difficult to candle
due to their colour.
Turning   treated the same as Ostrich
Hatching   as Ostrich
Hatching Temperature   set @ 1°C lower than the incubation temperature   35.0°C
Humidity   32.0°C wet bulb reading = 80% RH
Brooding   treated as Ostrich

227

The afore-mentioned information is only designed as a general guide to the requirements of each species. If a commercial project is planned, a more detailed review of the requirements should be undertaken with an expert in the field.

PARROTS

Included under the term Parrots, are the following species: Macaws, Cockatoos, Amazons and African Parrots, Parakeets, Lories, Lorikeets and Parrotlets.

In recent years the world has become aware that the natural habitat for parrot-like species is being lost at an alarming rate. The ever increasing demand for wild caught specimens for the pet trade has resulted in restrictions being imposed on the export of these species from their native countries. This has led to a major swing to captive breeding, with the accompanying need for artificial incubation. As so many of these species are rare and endangered, the need to increase the captive population has now become very important. In order to ensure the best possible hatch, incubation techniques using weight loss and density techniques are in increasing use.

Research has shown that the porosity of parrot eggs can vary. Consequently frequent monitoring and adjustment of the humidity levels needs to be done to ensure that moisture loss is on target.

Incubation   temperature (moving air)   36.8° - 37.0°C
              humidity   wet bulb reading 24.5° - 26.6°C = 36% - 44% RH

(In areas of high ambient humidity, it is advisable to run an incubator dry to obtain the lowest RH, even though some birds may incubate in high humidity in their native habitats).

If the incubator is still recording a higher than acceptable RH, other ways of reducing it must be sought. One is to reduce the temperature in the incubation room; remember that the higher the temperature, the higher the humidity is likely to be. If reducing the ambient temperature in the room is not possible, the use of an electric dehumidifier is advisable; this will actually extract the moisture from the air and turn it into water which is held within the dehumidifier.

Egg washing is a practice undertaken by many breeders prior to setting in an incubator. It is most important to remember to use a well-tried egg dip. Several are now available on the market, in small quantities, suitable for the breeder with a limited number of birds. When an egg wash is used, all the natural protection against bacteria put on the shell of the egg when laid is also lost. Therefore it is important to handle eggs cautiously during incubation. Gloves should be used, or at least your hands should be washed with an antiseptic solution, since dirty or contaminated hands will quickly infect the unprotected eggs.

There are several turning methods used for parrot eggs. Eggs may be placed on their sides on rollers, rolled on a moving base between holding rods, or placed vertically in plastic trays and turned through 90°.

All these methods have their partial merits. If the egg is allowed to remain on its side through out incubation there is a possibility that the chick, when turning within the egg prior to hatching, will try to come out the wrong end and fail to hatch. A number of breeders have now adopted the practice of placing their eggs on suitable rollers for the first 10 - 15 days. When the membrane growth has reached the pointed end of the egg, the egg is placed in a plastic insert and turned vertically through 90° until internal pip is observed. This method has two advantages. The chick is now in a position to pip at the correct end and more eggs can be incubated at the same time in a vertical position. Experience has shown that Macaw and Cockatoo eggs need to be started on their sides, Other species, such as African Grey parrots, will successfully incubate to pipping placed vertically in inserts. It is thought that Macaw and Cockatoo eggs have smaller yolks than other species' eggs of comparable size and have some difficulty with membrane growth if started vertically.

hatching	temperature	dry bulb reading @ 36.8 - 36.9°C
	humidity	wet bulb reading @31.0° - 32°C = 65-70% RH

Once the egg has internally pipped, it is placed in a small open-topped container in the hatcher. When the chick has hatched and is dry it can be placed in a brooder.

An old plastic ice-cream container with the bottom cut out can retain the hatched chick in one area of the hatcher. (Plastic fruit punnets used by supermarkets can also fulfill the same function and sometimes have the advantage of already being perforated with a number of holes to allow easy ventilation.) Care should be taken to ensure no sharp edges are left on the plastic when it is cut. This also allows different species to be hatched at the same time without getting mixed up.

PENGUINS

Many zoos and wildlife parks that keep penguins are now trying to breed from their colonies, but as yet not too much information has been published on their experiences of captive breeding. For those embarking on artificial incubation, the foregoing must be regarded as only a guide, with precise details being obtained from successful breeders.

Artificial incubation		Varies between 31 - 56 days
	(for specific incubation periods see Appendix 1)	
Incubation	temperature (moving air)	dry bulb reading 36.5°C
	humidity	wet bulb reading 29.5°C = 60% RH
Weight loss	should be around 15%	

If the cuticle is washed off with a good poultry egg wash prior to the start of incubation, this can give a further 16% shell conductance as has been found with King Penguin eggs. This could well be a useful procedure in the future for all eggs which have a thick cuticle layer, thus ensuring a high functional porosity for respiratory gas exchange to achieve the required weight loss and a successful hatch.

Turning

Turning is probably the most important factor required for the successful incubation of penguin eggs. Unlike turkeys and other species with eggs of a similar size, the penguin egg has a larger amount of albumen in relation to the yolk and, from experience, requires to be turned more often.

In the case of automatic turning incubators, the eggs are places on their sides, secured in a basket or holder and turned every hour through 90°. In addition, each egg is inverted by hand 7 times a day. This additional turning has been found to be successful with Humboldt Penguins. Should the incubator in use have turning rollers rather than holding trays, ensure that each roller is large enough in diameter to rotate the egg in question through at least 180°.

Hatching

At internal pip, place the eggs into a moving air hatcher on their sides; no turning is required. The hatcher having been set up at 36.0°C dry bulb, with wet bulb at 29.0°C = 60% RH. Once the chicks are hatched and dry, they are placed in a brooder at a temperature of 35.0°C, reducing by 1° each day for the next 6 days.

BIRDS OF PREY

The term *Birds of Prey* covers all the Falcons, Hawks, Owls, and Eagles. As a group they all require a similar sort of treatment for incubation and hatching. Egg freshness is always an important factor with this order and the laying dates should be carefully monitored. Eggs should be marked and stored on their sides whilst waiting for incubation.

They should be turned through 180° twice a day, and stored at a room temperature of around 12.5°C. Should any of the eggs be dirty when taken from the nest, the contamination can either be removed using fine sandpaper or, in bad cases, washed with a poultry egg wash. But remember - once the cuticle (the protective coating put on the outside of the egg when the egg is laid) is removed, the egg is open to any bacteria around, and therefore it is advisable to use gloves when handling the eggs after this point.

Artificial incubation	For specific incubation periods see Appendix I	
Incubation	temperature (moving air), dry bulb reading	37.5°C
	humidity, wet bulb reading	25.5° - 27°C = 40 - 45%RH
	(for thin shelled eggs: Merlins, Kestrels, Owls)	
	humidity, wet bulb reading	28.0°C = 50% RH
Hatching	temperature (moving –air), dry bulb reading	36.5°C
	humidity, wet bulb reading	30.5°C = 66% RH

The above temperatures and humidities are a general guide, since many breeders now use egg weighing as a method of judging the humidity required during incubation. Once the eggs show they are internally pipped, they are placed in a hatcher. The time from pip to hatch can take between 36 and 48 hours with most species, but individual eggs may require up to 72 hours. Hatching times of less than 24 and more than 80 hours usually signify trouble. Once an egg has started to chip, it should be left untouched until it has hatched.

Always resist premature help, as more chicks are damaged by interference than by any other cause. When the chick is out of the egg, remove it from the hatcher immediately and dust the umbilicus with antibiotic powder. Place the chick in a brooder box with a temperature around 36.5°C in the centre so it can move out to the side should it wish to move to a cooler temperature. The floor of the brooder must have a covering that is made of an uneven and non-slip material; this will help to prevent splayed legs.

REPTILES

Unlike avian species, reptile eggs do not require to be turned and their temperature is lower during incubation. Temperature and humidity are the most important factors when artificially incubating reptile eggs, as in some species the sex of the hatchings can be determined by the temperature at which the eggs are incubated. For success with artificial incubation, an incubator which can hold its temperature and humidity over a long period at a set level is best for the purpose. This is usually achieved by using one of the latest moving air models, which also has automatic humidity control.

This section covers a range of species which include Turtles, Tortoise, Lizards, Snakes and Crocodiles. Having such a large number of species within each order, it is impossible to cover each one, so for the purposes of a general guide a cross section is being taken for reference. The general practice by most breeders is to place reptile eggs in a plastic container, with a loose fitting or perforated lid to allow in a little air, but retaining a high level of humidity. This container is then put in an incubator with its own high level of humidity around 80% RH.

The eggs are placed in various types of substrate depending on the breeder's choice and also the natural environment of the species concerned. Vermiculite, peat moss, or sand is generally used. The eggs are submersed in a substrate up to approx $^1/_3$rd of their depth, and placed 2 - 3cm apart, as reptile eggs generally increase in size during incubation. A degree of water is added to the substrate before incubation to obtain a starting humidity. Additional sterile warm water can be sprinkled on the substrate during incubation should it become dried out.

VENEZUELAN SLIDES TURTLE

Incubation period   56 - 72 days
Suggested substrate   vermiculite - mix 2:1 with water
Incubation   temperature, dry bulb reading
                                             28.0° - 29.0°C
                     humidity, wet bulb reading   26.0°C = 80% RH
Sex ratio   1:1

When hatched, place in individual warm, moist, darkened containers until the yolk-sac is fully absorbed, then transfer to an aquaria, time scale 1- 7 days.

GALAPAGOS TORTOISE

Incubation period   91 - 112 days
Suggested substrate   vermiculite and peat moss mixed at rate 1:1 and slightly
                                dampened for moisture. Eggs half buried in substrate approx
                                4cm apart.
Incubation   temperature, dry bulb reading   27.0° - 29.0°C
                     humidity, wet bulb reading   24.5° - 26.5°C = 80%RH

These temperatures will produce both sexes. When hatched, transfer to semi-darkened cabinet, between 28.0°-30.0°C with corrugated paper as substrate that allows air to circulate under the plastron to aid yolk absorption. Hatchlings begin to feed in approximately *5* days.

AFRICAN SPURRED TORTOISE

Incubation period   81 - 170 days
Suggested substrate   vermiculite and water at the rate by weight, 2:1 ratio. Eggs

                                submerged $^1/_3$rd in substrate 2 - 3cm apart.
Incubation   temperature, dry bulb reading   29.0° - 32.0°C
                     humidity, wet bulb reading   26.0° - 29.0°C = 80% RH

Leave each hatchling in a darkened heated contained until its yolk-sac is absorbed, and placed on a dampened paper towel; this will help to avoid damage to the yolk-sac during this period. Once the yolk-sac is absorbed, place the hatchlings in a box with temperature at one end at 28.0°C. This enables each hatchling to select somewhere within the box that suits its own temperature requirement.

LEOPARD TORTOISE

Incubation period   155 - 176 days
Suggested substrate   moist sand (moisten only when the sand is completely dry)
Incubation   temperature, dry bulb reading   27.0° - 30.0°C
                                 humidity, wet bulb reading   24.5° - 27.5°C = 80% RH

Hatchlings can be seen pipping their eggs 1 - 2 days before they actually hatch, and the yolk-sac is usually absorbed within 4 - 6 days. Place the hatchlings in a container with a substrate of moist peat, heated at one end to a temperature of 35.0°C and 22.0°C at the other.

NAMIB GECKO

Incubation period   70 days
Suggested substrate   vermiculite mixed with water in a ratio 4:1 by weight
Incubation   temperature, dry bulb reading   28.0° - 32.0°C
                                 humidity, wet bulb reading   23.5° - 25°C = 55 - 60% RH

Immediately the gecko hatches it will begin to slough and should be left in the incubator until the process is complete. Care should be taken not to put these hatchlings under too much stress in the early stages of their lives. Young will start to feed 2-3 days after the hatch.

FIJIAN CRESTED IGUANA

Incubation period
                                                                       147 - 210 days
Suggested substrate   vermiculite or sphagnum moss
slightly moistened. Eggs   placed 4cm apart on top of the
                                                                       substrate
Incubation   temperature, dry bulb reading   27.0° - 30.0°C
                                 humidity, wet bulb reading   23.0° - 25.5°C = 65 - 75% RH

Place hatchlings in a semi-darkened container until their yolk-sac is absorbed.

WEST INDIAN ROCK IGUANA

Incubation period   98 days
Suggested substrate   vermiculite kept moist
Incubation   temperature, dry bulb reading   28.0° - 30.0°C
                                 humidity, wet bulb reading   24.5° - 27.0°C = 75%- 80% RH

Fertility can be observed approx 2 weeks into incubation. Eggs that develop mould or are not fertile must be removed immediately. On hatching the hatchlings should be placed in a semi-darkened box until the yolk-sac is completed absorbed; after *5* days light can then be increased and food offered.

KOMODO MONITOR LIZARD

Incubation period		145 days
Suggested substrate	corrugated paper, sand/peat. One successful method is to place each egg in a small ball of moistened peat. Fertility can be noted at 2 weeks into incubation.	
Incubation	temperature, dry bulb reading	28.0°C
	humidity, wet bulb reading	25.0° - 26.0°C = 80% - 85%RH

ROCK PYTHON

Incubation period		76 - 88 days
Suggested substrate	vermiculite moistened	
Incubation	temperature, dry bulb reading	30.0°C
	humidity, wet bulb reading	27.0°C = 80%RH

AMERICAN ALLIGATORS

Incubation period		2 - 3 months
Suggested substrate	moistened vermiculite	
Incubation	temperature can be varied to determining the sexes required. If eggs are incubated at 29.0°-30.0°C it is likely that most of the hatchlings will be female. Conversely if the eggs are incubated at 33.0° - 34.0°C they will be mainly males.	

The critical period for temperature sex determination (TSD) is early in the incubation process. Extending from the 7th to the 21st day, failure of eggs to hatch can be caused by too high or low temperatures, I.e. above 34.0°C or below 27.0°C

humidity, wet-bulb reading 26 - 27°C or 30 - 30.5°C = 85% RH

After hatching the hatchlings are placed in plastic containers, gently sloping, with a little water covering up to about one third of the floor. The hatchlings begin to feed in about 3 weeks, after the yolk sac is absorbed.

As previously mentioned, the above information is only intended as a guide, and those who are interested in serious breeding should contact their local Herpetological or Zoological Society for further guidance.

APPENDIX 1

INCUBATION PERIODS
GROUPS OF SPECIES LISTED IN ALPHABETICAL ORDER

Amazon Parrots	Days	Kea	Days
Blue fronted	26	Kea	28-29
Cuban	26 - 28	Kites	
Green-cheeked	24	Brahminy	26-27
Hispaniolan	25	Black Winged	25-28
Lilac-crowned	26	Red	31-32
Puerto Rican	25 - 26	Kookaburra	
Spectacled	24	Laughing	25
Yellow-naped	28 - 29	Blue-winged	23-24
White-fronted	24 - 25	Plovers	
Avocets		Lapwing	24-26
American	22 - 24	Spur-winged	22-24
Common	22 - 24	Blk Band Sand	24-25
Buzzards		Black Bellied	23
Common	33 - 38	Blacksmith	26
Honey	30 - 35	Crowned	25
Long-legged	28	Dotterel	21
Rough-legged	31	Golden	30
Bustards		Greater Sand	23-25
Great	25 - 28	Kentish	24
Little	20 - 21	Killdeer	28
Houbara	20 - 21	Kittlitz's Sand	23-26
Capercaillie		Little Ringed	22
Black-billed	24	Piping	27-31
Common	24 - 28	Ringed	22
Caracara		Wattled	30-32
Crested	28	Kiwi	
Cockatiel		Kiwi	75-80
Cockatiel	18-20	Lorikeets	
Cockatoos		Fairy	25
Bare-eyed	23-24	Goldie's	24
Blue-eyed	30	Johnson's	21-23
Black	28	Little	22
Citron crested	25-26	Masena's	23-26
Galah	22-24	Meyer's	23-24
Gang Gang	30	Musk	25
Glossy	29	Ornate	26-28
Goffin's	25	Purple-Crown	22
Gtr. Sulphur	27-28	Red-flanked	25
Leadbeater's	26	Scaly Breasted	23

236

	24-25	Stella's	26-27
Med Sulphur	26-27	Swainson's	25-26
Moluccan	28-29	Varied	22
Palm	28-30	Weber's	27
Phil Red-vent	24	*Lories*	
Red-tail Black	30	Black	25-27
Slender-billed	23-24	Black-capped	24
Umbrella	28	Blue-crowned	23
Conures		Chattering	26
Blue-crowned	23	Collared	30
Blue-throated	24-26	Dusky	24
Brown-throated	23	Duyvenbode's	24
Dusky-headed	23	Ornate	27
Green-cheeked	22-24	Papuan	21
Nanday	21-23	Rainbow	25-26
Orange-fronted	30	Red Moluccan	24
Patagonian	24-25	Tahitian	25
Pearly	25	Violet-necked	27
Sun	28	Yellow backed	24
White-eared	27	*Lovebirds*	
Cranes		Black-cheeked	24
Australian	35-36	Black-winged	25
Black-necked	31-33	Fischer's	23
Cana. Sandhill	27	Grey-headed	23
Common	28-31	Masked	23
Crowned	28-31	Nyasa	22
Demoiselle	27-30	Peach-faced	23
Flori. Sandhill	31-32	Red-faced	22
Gtr. Sandhill	31-32	*Macaws*	
Japanese	30-34	Blue & Gold	26
Sarus	28	Buffin's	26-27
Siberian White	29	Caninde	26
Stanley	29-30	Chestnut-front	28
Wattled	35-40	Green-winged	26
White-naped	28-32	Hyacinth	26-28
Whooping	30	Illiger's	26-27
Curlews		Military	26
Eurasian	29	Red-bellied	25
Long-billed	30	Red-fronted	26
Stone	21-23	Red-shoulder	24
Whimbrel	27	Scarlet	26
Ducks		Yellow-collared	26
African Black	28	*Owls*	
Amer. Widgeon	26	Barn	32-34
Aus.Grey Teal	26	Great Horned	35
Aus. White-eye	26	Hawk	26-30
Baer's Pochard	27	Little Scops	24-25
Bahama Pintail	26	Snowy	33-36
Baikal Teal	26	Tawny	28-30
Barrow's G'eye	30	*Parakeets*	
Black Scoter	28	Bourke's	18
Blue-wing Teal	26	Blue-winged	18
Brazilian Teal	26	Red-rumped	20

Appendix 1   Incubation times

Bronze Winged	30	Elegant	18
Canvasback	26	Orange-bellied	20-21
Cape Teal	26	Rock	18
Chestnut Breastd	26	Turquoise	18
Chilean Teal	26	Splendid	18
Chiloe Widgeon.	26	Swift	20
Chin. Spotbill	28	Alexandrine	26-27
Cinnamon Teal	26	Barred	18
Comb Duck	30	Canary-winged	26
Com. Shoveler	26	Derbyan	26
Com.White-eye	26	Quaker	23
Crested Duck	30	Red-fronted	20
Cuban Tree	30	Rose-ringed	23-24
Euro Eider	27	Long-tailed	24
Euro Goldeneye	28	Malabar	27
Euro Pochard	27	Moustached	25-26
White-wg Scoter	28	Sierra	28
Euro Widgeon	26	Yellow-fronted	20
Eyton's Whistling	30	Ringneck	20
Falcated Teal	26	*Parrots*	
Florida Duck	28	African Grey	28
Fulvous Tree	28	Amboina King	20
Gadwall	26	Australian Ring	20-21
Garganey	24	Blue Bonnets	19
Goosander	30	Blue Headed	24-27
Greater Scaup	28	Brown-headed	26
Green-wing Teal	25	Eclectus	28
Grey Duck	28	Gold-shoulder	19
Harlequin Duck	30	Green-wg King	20
Hartlaub's Duck	32	Hawk-headed	28
Hawaiian Duck	28	Jardine's	25-26
Hooded Mergan	28	Meyer's	24-25
HottentotTeal	25	Paradise	21
Indian Spotbill	26	Pesquet's	26-29
Javan Tree Duck	28	Pileated	24
Kerguelen Pintail	26	Princess	20
Laysan Teal	28	Rock	18
Lesser Scaup	27	Senegal	24-25
Longtail Duck	23	S.A .Red-cap	23
Mallard	28	Superb	20
Maned Goose	30	Timneh Grey	26
Mandarin Duck	28	White-capped	26-28
Marbled Teal	26	*Hanging Parrots*	
N.Z.Brown Teal	28	Ceylon	19
N.Z.Scaup	26	Double-eye Fig	18-19
N.Z.Shoveler	26	Phillipine Hang	20
N.America Black	27	Salvadori's Fig	23
N.America Ruddy	24	Vernal Hanging	22
N.America Wood	28	Pacific	17
Northern Pintail	26	*Penguins*	
Philippine Duck	26	Adelie	33-38
Puna Teal	26	Emperor	62-64
Radjah Shelduck	30	Humbolt	36-42

Red-billed Pintail	26	King	51-57
Red-billed Tree	28	Gentoo	31-39
Red Breast Merg	30	Chinstrap	34-40
Redcrest P'chard	28	Fiordland	31-36
Redhead	28	Snares	31-37
Ring Teal	24	Rockhopper	32-34
Ringneck	26	Royal	32-37
Sharpwing Teal	26	Yellow-eyed	39-51
Com Shelduck	30	Macaroni	33-40
Smew	28	Little	33-37
Southern P'chard	26	Jackass	38
Spectacled Eider	24	Magellanic	38-42
Spotted Tree	31	Galapagos	38-42
Tufted Duck	26	*Pelicans*	
Versicolor Teal	30	Brown	28-29
Wandering Tree	30	White	29-30
White-faced Tree	28	*Partridges*	
Yellowbill Duck	27	Grey	23-25
African Crowned	49	Red-legged	23-25
African Fish	44-45	Rock	24-26
Bald	35	Chukar	23
Batleur	42-43	Barbary	25
Black	43-46	See See	21
Bonelli's	37-40	Sand	21
Booted	36-38	Common Hill	24
Golden	43-45	Rufous-throat	20-21
Imperial	43	White-throated	20-21
Lesser Spotted	38-41	Javan Hill	24
Martial	45	Brown-breast	26
Short-toed	45-47	Sumatran Hill	24
Spotted	42-44	Chin. Bamboo	18
Steepe	64-66	Mount.Bamboo	18-19
White-tailed	34-42	Ferruginous W	18-20
Egrets		Madagascan	16-18
Cattle	24	Crimson-head	18-19
Great White	25	Black Wood	18-19
Intermediate	21	Daurian	26
Little	21-25	Tibetan	24-26
Falcons		Stone	22
Eleanora's	28	Long-billed	18-19
Gyr	35	Roulroul	18
Lanner	32-35	TibetSnowcock	27-28
Prairie	31	Himl.Snowcock	27-28
Saker	30	*Pheasants*	
Geese		Lady Amherst	23
Abyssin Bluewing	31	Blood	28
Andean	30	Blue-eared	26-28
Ashy-headed	30	Blyth's Trag	28
Atlantic Brent	23	Brown-eared	26-27
Bar-headed	28	Bronze-tailed	22
Barnacle	28	Bulwer's	25
Black Brent	23	Cabot's Trag	28
Canada	28	Cheer	26

Cereopsis	35	Common	24-25
Cackling Canada	28	CongoPeacock	28
Dusky Canada	28	Copper	24-25
Eastern Greylag	28	Crested Argus	25
Egyptian	30	Crested FB	24
Emperor	25	Crestless FB.	23-24
Euro White-front	26	Edwards'	21-24
Giant Canada	28	Elliot's	25
Hawaiian	29	Germain's PP	22
Kelp	32	Golden	23
Less. White-front	25	Great Argus	24-25
Magellan	30	Grey PP	22
Moffitt's Canada	28	Green	24-25
Orinoco	30	Himal. Monal	28
Pinkfoot	28	Hume's BT	27-28
Red-breasted	25	Imperial	25
Ross's	23	Kalij	23-25
Ruddy Headed	30	Koklass	21-22
Russian Bean	28	Malayan PP	22
Snow	25	Mikado	26-28
Spur-winged	32	Palawan	18-19
Swan	28	Mountain PP	22
Taverner's Can	28	Blue Peafowl	28
Western Bean	28	Reeve's	24-25
Western Greylag	28	Salvadori's	22
Whitefront	26	Satyr Trag	28
Vancouver Can	28	Siamese FB	24-25
Godwits		Silver	25
Bar-tailed	24	Swinhoe's	25
Black-tailed	24	Temmin. Trag	28
Marbled	24	Western Trag	28
Hudsonian	24	White-eared	24
Grouse		*Prairie Chicken*	
Black	26-27	Greater	24-25
Blue	24-25	Lesser	25-26
Hazel	25	*Ptarmigan*	
Ruffed	24	Rock	21
Sage	25-27	White-tailed	22-23
Sharptailed	24-25	*Quail*	
Spruce	21	Barred	22-23
Red/Willow	21-22	Bearded Tree	28-30
Harriers		Blk.Throat. BW	24
Hen	29-31	Northern BW	22
Marsh	31-38	Brown	18
Montagu's	27-30	Californian	22-23
Pallid	29-30	Chinese Paint	16
Hawks		Crested	23
Red-tailed	28-32	Elegant	22
Goshawk	35-38	Eurasian	17-20
Sparrow	30-31	Gambel's	22
Hobby	28-31	Harlequin	16-18
Osprey	35-38	Japanese	18
Kestrel	28-29	Jungle Bush	21

Herons			Mearn's	24-25
Black Headed	25		Painted Bush	21
Capped	26-27		Rain	18-19
Chinese	18-22		Scaled	22-23
Cocoi	24-26		Spot-winged W	26-27
Eastern Reef	25-28		Stubble	18-21
Goliath	28		**Roller**	
Great Blue	28		Eurasian	18-19
Grey	25-26		**Storks**	
Indian Pond	24		Open-billed	24-25
Japanese Night	17-20		Black	30-35
Little Blue	21-23		Hammerhead	30
Malagasy Pond	20		Marabou	30
BkCrowned Night	21-22		**Swans**	
Purple	26		Bewick's	30
Rufescent Tiger	31-34		Black	36
Squacco	22-24		Black-necked	36
Tricoloured	21		Coscoroba	35
White Back Night	24-26		Mute	37
White Faced	24-26		Trumpeter	33
Yellow Crn Night	21-25		Whistling	36
Ibis			Whooper	33
Bald	24-25		**Vultures**	
Glossy	21		Bearded	55-60
Hadada	26		Egyptian	42
Japanese Crest	30		King	56-58
Northern Bald	27-28		Black	55
Oriental	23-25		White-backed	50
Scarlet	21-23		Griffon	52
Sacred	28-29		**Waders**	
Jacana			Redshank	23-24
American	22-25		Ruff	27
Jay			Com. Snipe	20
Eurasian	16-17		Blk-wing Stilt	24-27
Siberian	18-20		Temm.Stilt	20
Jungle Fowl			Thick-knees	24
Ceylon	20-21		Whimbrel	27
Green	21		Afri. Spoonbill	23-24
Grey	20-21		Euro Spoonbill	25
Red	19-21			

A simple guide to specific problems when incubating eggs

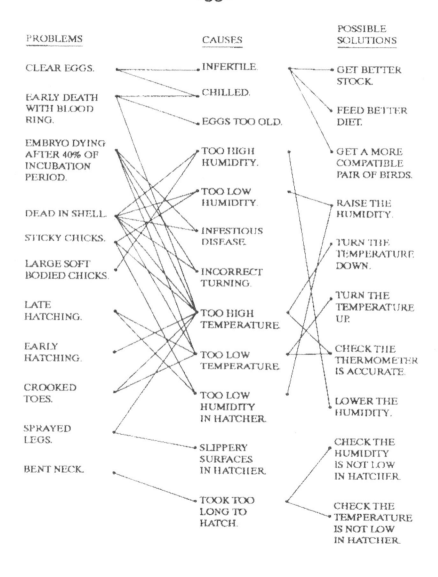

PROBLEMS	CAUSES	POSSIBLE SOLUTIONS
CLEAR EGGS.	INFERTILE.	GET BETTER STOCK.
EARLY DEATH WITH BLOOD RING.	CHILLED.	FEED BETTER DIET.
	EGGS TOO OLD.	
EMBRYO DYING AFTER 40% OF INCUBATION PERIOD.	TOO HIGH HUMIDITY.	GET A MORE COMPATIBLE PAIR OF BIRDS.
	TOO LOW HUMIDITY.	RAISE THE HUMIDITY.
DEAD IN SHELL.	INFESTIOUS DISEASE.	
STICKY CHICKS.		TURN THE TEMPERATURE DOWN.
LARGE SOFT BODIED CHICKS.	INCORRECT TURNING.	
LATE HATCHING.	TOO HIGH TEMPERATURE.	TURN THE TEMPERATURE UP.
EARLY HATCHING.	TOO LOW TEMPERATURE.	CHECK THE THERMOMETER IS ACCURATE.
CROOKED TOES.	TOO LOW HUMIDITY IN HATCHER.	LOWER THE HUMIDITY.
SPRAYED LEGS.	SLIPPERY SURFACES IN HATCHER.	CHECK THE HUMIDITY IS NOT LOW IN HATCHER.
BENT NECK.		
	TOOK TOO LONG TO HATCH.	CHECK THE TEMPERATURE IS NOT LOW IN HATCHER.

Fahrenheit - Centigrade Conversion Table

F	C	F	C	F	C
32.0	0.0	57.0	13.8	82.0	27.8
32.5	0.3	57.5	14.1	82.5	28.0
33.0	0.6	58.0	14.4	83.0	28.3
33.5	0.8	58.5	14.7	83.5	28.6
34.0	1.1	59.0	15.0	84.0	28.9
34.5	1.4	59.5	15.2	84.5	29.1
35.0	1.7	60.0	15.5	85.0	29.4
35.5	1.9	60.5	15.8	85.5	29.7
36.0	2.2	61.0	16.1	86.0	30.0
36.5	2.5	61.5	16.4	86.5	30.2
37.0	2.8	62.0	16.7	87.0	30.5
37.5	3.1	62.5	16.9	87.5	30.8
38.0	3.3	63.0	17.2	88.0	31.1
38.5	3.6	63.5	17.5	88.5	31.4
39.0	3.9	64.0	17.8	89.0	31.6
39.5	4.2	64.5	18.0	89.5	31.9
40.0	4.4	65.0	18.3	90.0	32.2
40.5	4.7	65.5	18.6	90.5	32.5
41.5	5.3	66.5	19.1	91.5	33.0
42.0	5.6	67.0	19.4	92.0	33.3
42.5	5.8	67.5	19.7	92.5	33.6
43.0	6.1	68.0	20.0	93.0	33.9
43.5	6.4	68.5	20.3	93.5	34.1
44.0	6.7	69.0	20.5	94.0	34.4
44.5	6.9	69.5	20.8	94.5	34.7
45.0	7.2	70.0	21.1	95.0	35.0
45.5	7.5	70.5	21.4	95.5	35.2
46.0	7.8	71.0	21.6	96.0	35.5
46.5	8.0	71.5	21.9	96.5	35.8
47.0	8.3	72.0	22.2	97.0	36.1
47.5	8.6	72.5	22.5	97.5	36.4
48.0	8.9	73.0	22.8	98.0	36.6
48.5	9.2	73.5	23.0	98.5	36.9
49.0	9.4	74.0	23.3	99.0	37.2
49.5	9.7	74.5	23.6	99.5	37.5
50.0	10.0	75.0	23.9	100.0	37.7
50.5	10.3	75.5	24.1	100.5	38.0
51.0	10.5	76.0	24.4	101.0	38.3
51.5	10.8	76.5	24.7	101.5	38.6
52.0	11.1	77.0	25.0	102.0	38.9
52.5	11.4	77.5	25.3	102.5	39.1
53.0	11.7	78.0	25.5	103.0	39.4
53.5	11.9	78.5	25.8	103.5	39.7
54.0	12.2	79.0	26.1	104.0	40.0
54.5	12.5	79.5	26.4	104.5	40.2
55.0	12.8	80.0	26.6	105.0	40.5
55.5	13.0	80.5	26.9	105.5	40.8
56.0	13.3	81.0	27.2	106.0	41.1
56.5	13.6	81.5	27.5	106.5	41.3

Appendix 1 Dry / Wet Bulb Conversion Table

Conversion Table   Wet-bulb reading - % Relative Humidity

Dry Bulb Temperature

Wet Bulb Celcius	AVIAN				REPTILIAN										
	37.5	37.0	36.5	36.0	33.0	32.5	32.0	31.5	31.0	30.5	30.0	29.5	29.0	28.5	28.0
37.5	%	%	%	%	%	%	%	%	%	%	%	%	%	%	%
37.0	97														
36.5	93	97													
36.0	90	93	97												
35.5	87	90	93	97											
35.0	84	87	90	93											
34.5	81	84	87	90											
34.0	78	81	84	87											
33.5	75	78	81	84											
33.0	72	75	78	81											
32.5	69	72	75	78	97										
32.0	67	69	72	75	93	97									
31.5	64	67	69	72	90	93	97								
31.0	61	64	67	69	87	90	93	96							
30.5	59	61	64	66	83	86	90	93	96						
30.0	56	59	61	63	80	83	86	90	93	96					
29.5	54	56	59	61	77	80	83	86	90	93	96				
29.0	52	54	56	58	74	77	80	83	86	90	93	96			
28.5	50	52	54	55	71	74	77	80	83	86	89	96	96		
28.0	47	50	51	53	69	71	74	77	80	83	86	93	93	96	
27.5	45	47	50	52	66	68	71	73	77	80	83	89	89	93	96
27.0	43	45	48	51	63	65	68	70	73	77	79	86	86	89	93
26.5	41	43	45	48	60	62	65	67	70	73	76	82	82	85	89
26.0	39	41	44	46	58	60	62	64	67	70	73	79	79	82	85
25.5	37	39	41	44	55	57	60	62	64	67	70	76	76	79	82
25.0	35	37	39	42	52	54	57	59	62	64	67	72	72	75	79
24.5	33	35	37	40	50	52	54	56	59	62	64	69	69	72	75
24.0	31	33	35	38	47	49	52	53	56	59	61	66	66	69	72
23.5	29	31	33	36	45	46	49	51	53	56	58	63	63	65	69
23.0	27	29	31	34	43	44	46	48	51	53	56	60	60	62	65
22.5	25	27	29	32	40	42	44	45	48	51	52	57	57	59	62
22.0	23	25	27	30	38	39	42	43	45	48	50	54	54	56	59
21.5	22	23	26	28	36	37	39	41	43	45	47	52	52	53	56
21.0	20	22	24	26	34	35	37	38	41	43	44	49	49	51	53
20.5	18	20	22	24	31	32	35	36	38	41	42	46	46	48	51
20.0	17	18	21	23	29	30	32	34	36	38	39	43	43	45	48
19.5			18	20	27	28	30	31	33	36	37	41	41	42	45
19.0				18	25	26	28	29	31	33	34	38	38	40	42
18.5					23	24	26	27	29	31	32	36	36	37	40
18.0					21	22	24	24	27	29	30	33	33	34	37
17.5					19	20	22	22	24	27	27	31	31	32	34
17.0					17	18	20	20	22	24	25	28	28	29	32
16.5					15	16	18	18	20	22	23	26	26	27	29
16.0					14	14	16	16	18	20	21	24	24	25	27

APPENDIX 2

GLOSSARY

Allantois The membrane that acts as the lungs and kidneys of the developing chick while the definitive organs are forming. It arises as an out growth of the hind gut, so acts as a depository for waste products as well.

Amnion The membrane that completely surrounds the developing chick, enclosing it in its own private pond of amniotic fluid. This fluid enables the chick to move around freely, besides acting as a reservoir of water.

Auricle Often called the atrium. The right and left auricles are chambers of the heart, receiving the blood from the veins, and passing it to the ventricles, which pump it back round the circulation.

Blastula The name given to an embryo in the very early stages of development.

Bursa A bursa is a space in the body tissues. The Bursa of Fabricius is the blind tube opening into the vent of immature birds, It closes in adult birds.

Chalazae The twisted coils of thick white or albumen that suspend the yolk from each end of the shell.

Chorion The membrane formed coincidently with the amnion. After formation it fuses with the developing allantois.

Chromosomes Vital parts of the cell nucleus, normally only seen as paired threads when the cell divides. the genes, the instruments of inheritance, are arranged along the chromosomes.

Cloaca The end part of the gut, into which open the ducts from the kidneys and reproductive organs. Often called the vent.

Cytoplasm The fluid contents of a cell.

Dominant genes If a characteristic such as feather colour, differs between the parents, the offspring are sometimes the same colour as only one of the parents. The gene responsible for this feather colour is said to be the dominant gene. The gene for the suppressed colour is said to be recessive.

Evert To open out, or turn inside out.

Fallopian Tube The tube leading from the ovary to the uterus, or womb.

Germinal Cells The cells within the reproductive organs that will develop to form the zygotes, ova and sperm.

Germinal Disc The disc of cells, attached to the yolk, formed by multiple division of the original fertilized ovum. It will develop into the chick.

Hormone A substance produced by one organ of the body that is carried round by the blood, to influence another organ.

Imprinting During the first few hours after hatching, the chick devotedly follows, and learns to recognise, its mother. In the absence of a natural mother, it will imprint on any suitably sized moving object, and follow this, be it a broody hen or a human being.

Inbreeding The mating together, over several generations, of close relations, such as brother/sister, father/daughter, etc.

Infundibulum The funnel shaped end of the oviduct that receives the yolk, when it is released from the ovary.

Interstitial Cells The cells between the tiny tubes of the testis. The tubes produce the sperm; the interstitial cells produce the chemical hormones.

Meiosis The specialized division of the reproductive cells, so that each daughter cell has only half the number of chromosomes of the original cell.

Mitosis The normal division and multiplication of cells, each daughter cell being identical to the original cell.

Oocyte A cell that will develop into an ovum, or egg.

Out-Breeding The mating of a totally unrelated individual, or strain, with individuals of a strain that had become too in-bred. The introduction of fresh blood.

Outcross As out-breeding, but referring to one particular mating.

Ovary The female primary reproductive organ. The yolk is formed in the ovary.

Oviduct The tube down which the yolk passes. In the upper parts albumen is secreted on to the yolk, and in the lower parts, the membranes and shell are added, It opens into the vent.

Ovotestis The primitive primary reproductive organ, containing elements of both male and female reproductive tissue.

Pituitary Gland A small gland at the base of the brain. Nervous impulses from the brain cause it to produce hormones that act on the other endocrine glands.

Recessive Gene That element of inheritance, which is normally suppressed, by a more dominant element. Where both parents possess these recessive genes an offspring may show this characteristic, in the absence of the usual characteristic.

Secondary Sexual Characteristics Characteristics of animals, which differ between the sexes, but excluding reproductive organs and their associated ducts and glands (e.g. wattles on cock birds; plumage differences).

Spermatocyte A small cell, one of many, living in the somniferous tubules of the testis that will develop into a sperm.

Tubule A small hollow tube.

Ventricle A muscular chamber of the heart that pumps the blood into the arteries. Mammals and birds have two ventricles, the left one pumping oxygenated blood to the body and the right one pumping the blood to the lungs to be re-oxygenated.

Vitaline Membrane The very thin membrane, or 'skin', surrounding the yolk.

INDEX

  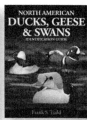 

Printed by Amazon Italia Logistica S.r.l.
Torrazza Piemonte (TO), Italy

11080590R00154